The Principles of

Naval Architecture Series

Vibration

William S. Vorus

J. Randolph Paulling, Editor

2010

Published by
The Society of Naval Architects
and Marine Engineers
601 Pavonia Avenue
Jersey City, New Jersey 07306

Library of Congress Cataloging-in-Publication Data

Vorus, William S.
  Vibration / William S. Vorus ; J. Randolph Paulling, editor.
     p. cm. — (The principles of naval architecture series)
  Includes bibliographical references and index.
  ISBN 978-0-939773-75-6
  1. Vibration (Marine engineering) 2. Naval architecture. I. Paulling, J. Randolph. II. Title.
  VM739.V67 2010
  623.8'171–dc22

                                                                            2010000496

                          ISBN 978-0-939773-75-6

                    Printed in the United States of America

                          First Printing, 2010

Table of Contents

An Introduction to the Series

The Society of Naval Architects and Marine Engineers is experiencing remarkable changes in the Maritime Industry as we enter our 115th year of service. Our mission, however, has not changed over the years . . . "an internationally recognized . . . technical society . . . serving the maritime industry, dedicated to advancing the art, science and practice of naval architecture, shipbuilding, ocean engineering, and marine engineering . . . encouraging the exchange and recording of information, sponsoring applied research . . . supporting education and enhancing the professional status and integrity of its membership."

In the spirit of being faithful to our mission, we have written and published significant treatises on the subject of naval architecture, marine engineering, and shipbuilding. Our most well known publication is the "Principles of Naval Architecture." First published in 1939, it has been revised and updated three times – in 1967, 1988, and now in 2008. During this time, remarkable changes in the industry have taken place, especially in technology, and these changes have accelerated. The result has had a dramatic impact on size, speed, capacity, safety, quality, and environmental protection.

The professions of naval architecture and marine engineering have realized great technical advances. They include structural design, hydrodynamics, resistance and propulsion, vibrations, materials, strength analysis using finite element analysis, dynamic loading and fatigue analysis, computer-aided ship design, controllability, stability, and the use of simulation, risk analysis and virtual reality.

However, with this in view, nothing remains more important than a comprehensive knowledge of "first principles." Using this knowledge, the Naval Architect is able to intelligently utilize the exceptional technology available to its fullest extent in today's global maritime industry. It is with this in mind that this entirely new 2008 treatise was developed – "The Principles of Naval Architecture: The Series." Recognizing the challenge of remaining relevant and current as technology changes, each major topical area will be published as a separate volume. This will facilitate timely revisions as technology continues to change and provide for more practical use by those who teach, learn or utilize the tools of our profession.

It is noteworthy that it took a decade to prepare this monumental work of nine volumes by sixteen authors and by a distinguished steering committee that was brought together from several countries, universities, companies and laboratories. We are all especially indebted to the editor, Professor J. Randolph (Randy) Paulling for providing the leadership, knowledge, and organizational ability to manage this seminal work. His dedication to this arduous task embodies the very essence of our mission . . . "to serve the maritime industry."

It is with this introduction that we recognize and honor all of our colleagues who contributed to this work.

Authors:

Dr. John S. Letcher	Hull Geometry
Dr. Colin S. Moore	Intact Stability
Robert D. Tagg	Subdivision and Damaged Stability
Professor Alaa Mansour and Dr. Donald Liu	Strength of Ships and Ocean Structures
Dr. Lars Larson and Dr. Hoyte Raven	Resistance
Professors Justin E. Kerwin and Jacques B. Hadler	Propulsion
Professor William S. Vorus	Vibration and Noise
Prof. Robert S. Beck, Dr. John Dalzell (Deceased), Prof. Odd Faltinsen and Dr. Arthur M. Reed	Motions in Waves
Professor W. C. Webster and Dr. Rod Barr	Controllability

Control Committee Members are:

Professor Bruce Johnson, Robert G. Keane, Jr., Justin H. McCarthy, David M. Maurer, Dr. William B. Morgan, Professor J. Nicholas Newman and Dr. Owen H. Oakley, Jr.

I would also like to recognize the support staff and members who helped bring this project to fruition, especially Susan Evans Grove, Publications Director, Phil Kimball, Executive Director, and Dr. Roger Compton, Past President.

In the new world's global maritime industry, we must maintain leadership in our profession if we are to continue to be true to our mission. The "Principles of Naval Architecture: The Series," is another example of the many ways our Society is meeting that challenge.

ADMIRAL ROBERT E. KRAMEK
Past President (2007–2008)

Foreword

Since it was first published 70 years ago, *Principles of Naval Architecture* (PNA) has served as a seminal text on naval architecture for both practicing professionals and students of naval architecture. This is a challenging task – to explain the fundamentals in terms understandable to the undergraduate student while providing sufficient rigor to satisfy the needs of the experienced engineer – but the initial publication and the ensuing revisions have stood the test of time. We believe that this third revision of PNA will carry on the tradition, and continue to serve as an invaluable reference to the marine community.

In the Foreword to the second revision of PNA, the Chairman of its Control Committee, John Nachtsheim, lamented the state of the maritime industry, noting that there were ". . . too many ships chasing too little cargo," and with the decline in shipping came a ". . . corresponding decrease in technological growth." John ended on a somewhat optimistic note: "Let's hope the current valley of worldwide maritime inactivity won't last for too long. Let's hope for better times, further technological growth, and the need once more, not too far away, for the next revision of *Principles of Naval Architecture*."

Fortunately, better times began soon after the second revision of PNA was released in 1988. Spurred by the expanding global economy and a trend toward specialization of production amongst nations around the world, seaborne trade has tripled in the last 20 years. Perhaps more than ever before, the economic and societal well being of nations worldwide is dependent upon efficient, safe, and environmentally friendly deep sea shipping. Continuous improvement in the efficiency of transportation has been achieved over the last several decades, facilitating this growth in the global economy by enabling lower cost movement of goods. These improvements extend over the entire supply train, with waterborne transportation providing the critical link between distant nations. The ship design and shipbuilding communities have played key roles, as some of the most important advancements have been in the design and construction of ships.

With the explosive growth in trade has come an unprecedented demand for tonnage extending over the full spectrum of ship types, including containerships, tankers, bulk carriers, and passenger vessels. Seeking increased throughput and efficiency, ship sizes and capacities have increased dramatically. Ships currently on order include 16,000 TEU containerships, 260,000 m^3 LNG carriers, and 5400 passenger cruise liners, dwarfing the prior generation of designs.

The drive toward more efficient ship designs has led to increased sophistication in both the designs themselves and in the techniques and tools required to develop the designs. Concepts introduced in Revision 2 of PNA such as finite element analysis, computational fluid dynamics, and probabilistic techniques for evaluating a ship's stability and structural reliability are now integral to the overall design process. The classification societies have released the common structural rules for tankers and bulk carriers, which rely heavily on first principles engineering, use of finite element analysis for strength and fatigue assessments, and more sophisticated approaches to analysis such as are used for ultimate strength assessment for the hull girder. The International Maritime Organization now relies on probabilistic approaches for evaluating intact and damage stability and oil outflow. Regulations are increasingly performance-based, allowing application of creative solutions and state-of-the-art tools. Risk assessment techniques have become essential tools of the practicing naval architect.

The cyclical nature of shipbuilding is well established and all of us who have weathered the ups and downs of the marine industry recognize the current boom will not last forever. However, there are reasons to believe that the need for technological advancement in the maritime industries will remain strong in the coming years. For example, naval architects and marine engineers will continue to focus on improving the efficiency of marine transportation systems, spurred by rising fuel oil prices and public expectations for reducing greenhouse gas emissions. As a consequence of climate change, the melting Arctic ice cap will create new opportunities for exploration and production of oil and other natural resources, and may lead to new global trading patterns.

SNAME has been challenged to provide technical updates to its texts on a timely basis, in part due to our reliance on volunteerism and in part due to the rapidly changing environment of the maritime industry. This revision of PNA emphasizes engineering fundamentals and first principles, recognizing that the methods and approaches for applying these fundamentals are subject to constant change. Under the leadership of President Bob Kramek, SNAME is reviewing all its publications and related processes. As the next SNAME President, one of my goals is to begin strategizing on the next revision of PNA just as this third revision comes off the presses. Comments and ideas you may have on how SNAME can improve its publications are encouraged and very much appreciated.

PNA would not be possible without the contributions of SNAME members and other marine professionals world-wide, who have advanced the science and the art of naval architecture and then shared their experiences through technical papers and presentations. For these many contributions we are indebted to all of you. We are especially indebted to its editor, Dr. J. Randolph Paulling, the Control Committee, the authors, and the reviewers who have given so generously of their time and expertise.

R. KEITH MICHEL
President (2009–2010)

Preface
Vibration

During the 20 years that have elapsed since publication of the previous edition of this book, there have been remarkable advances in the art, science, and practice of the design and construction of ships and other floating structures. In that edition, the increasing use of high speed computers was recognized and computational methods were incorporated or acknowledged in the individual chapters rather than being presented in a separate chapter. Today, the electronic computer is one of the most important tools in any engineering environment and the laptop computer has taken the place of the ubiquitous slide rule of an earlier generation of engineers.

Advanced concepts and methods that were only being developed or introduced then are a part of common engineering practice today. These include finite element analysis, computational fluid dynamics, random process methods, numerical modeling of the hull form and components, with some or all of these merged into integrated design and manufacturing systems. Collectively, these give the naval architect unprecedented power and flexibility to explore innovation in concept and design of marine systems. In order to fully utilize these tools, the modern naval architect must possess a sound knowledge of mathematics and the other fundamental sciences that form a basic part of a modern engineering education.

In 1997, planning for the new edition of *Principles of Naval Architecture* (PNA) was initiated by the SNAME publications manager who convened a meeting of a number of interested individuals including the editors of PNA and the new edition of *Ship Design and Construction* on which work had already begun. At this meeting it was agreed that PNA would present the basis for the modern practice of naval architecture and the focus would be *principles* in preference to *applications*. The book should contain appropriate reference material but it was not a handbook with extensive numerical tables and graphs. Neither was it to be an elementary or advanced textbook although it was expected to be used as regular reading material in advanced undergraduate and elementary graduate courses. It would contain the background and principles necessary to understand and to use intelligently the modern analytical, numerical, experimental, and computational tools available to the naval architect and also the fundamentals needed for the development of new tools. In essence, it would contain the material necessary to develop the understanding, insight, intuition, experience, and judgment needed for the successful practice of the profession. Following this initial meeting, a PNA Control Committee, consisting of individuals having the expertise deemed necessary to oversee and guide the writing of the new edition of PNA, was appointed. This committee, after participating in the selection of authors for the various chapters, has continued to contribute by critically reviewing the various component parts as they are written.

In an effort of this magnitude, involving contributions from numerous widely separated authors, progress has not been uniform and it became obvious before the halfway mark that some chapters would be completed before others. In order to make the material available to the profession in a timely manner it was decided to publish each major subdivision as a separate volume in the PNA series rather than treating each as a separate chapter of a single book.

Although the United States committed in 1975 to adopt SI units as the primary system of measurement the transition is not yet complete. In shipbuilding as well as other fields, we still find usage of three systems of units: English or foot-pound-seconds, SI or meter-newton-seconds, and the meter-kilogram(force)-second system common in engineering work on the European continent and most of the non-English speaking world prior to the adoption of the SI system. In the present work, we have tried to adhere to SI units as the primary system but other units may be found particularly in illustrations taken from other, older publications. The symbols and notation follow, in general, the standards developed by the International Towing Tank Conference.

This volume of the series presents the principles underlying analysis of the vibration characteristics of modern seagoing ships and the application of those principles in design and problem solving. The classical continuous beam model with steady state response to periodic excitation is presented first. This includes natural frequencies, mode shapes, and modal expansion. Discrete analysis is next presented based on finite element principles. Examples are discussed involving analysis of the entire ship and component parts (e.g., the deckhouse). The principal sources of excitation are usually the propulsion machinery and the propeller and methods of predicting the forces and moments produced by each are presented. There is a brief introduction to underwater acoustic radiation and sound as it is related to propeller effects.

Attention is devoted to design of the hull and propeller for vibration minimization. This includes design of the ship after body and appendages to ensure favorable wake characteristics, tip clearances, and selection of propeller characteristics such as number and shape of blades.

There are sections on vibration surveys, sea trials, acceptable vibration standards, and criteria. Concluding sections treat methods of remediation of vibration problems that are found after the ship is completed, including modifications to propeller design, structure, and machinery.

J. Randolph Paulling
Editor

Acknowledgments

The present volume, *Vibration*, could not have been completed without the assistance of a number of associates, colleagues, and former students who read and critiqued portions or all of the manuscript, helped with illustrations, tracked down references, and provided other vital services. William Vorus wishes especially to acknowledge the contributions of one of his graduate students, Mr. Aditya M. Aggarwal, who contributed to the proofreading and editing of the manuscript and to Mr. Ivan Zgaljic, Marine Engineering Section Head, AMSEC LLC, for a final review of the manuscript.

Special appreciation for the focused effort of Dr. Brandon Taravella of the School of NAME at the University of New Orleans for final correction and refinement of the chapter is expressed by the author and the SNAME staff.

Finally, the Editor extends his thanks to the author for his time and monumental efforts in writing the volume, to the Control Committee, and to the individuals listed above as well as others whose advice and assistance was essential to the successful completion of the task. He is especially grateful to Susan Evans, SNAME's Director of Publications, for her patience, ready advice, and close attention to detail without all of which this work could not have been accomplished.

Biography of William S. Vorus

Author of *Vibration*

William S. Vorus graduated with a BSME degree from Clemson University in 1963 and took an engineering job at Newport News Shipbuilding that same year. In 1968, he was sent to the University of Michigan, under both University and Shipyard financial support, where he was awarded an MSE degree in NAME in 1969 and a PhD in 1971. He returned to Newport News and resumed his engineering career in the Engineering Technical Department in 1971.

In 1973 he left the Shipyard and took a faculty position in the Department of NAME at the University of Michigan, where he achieved the rank full Professor in 1983. He authored Chapter 7, *Vibration*, in the previous PNA edition in 1989.

Vorus resigned his position at Michigan in 1996 to become the Chairman of the School of NAME at the University of New Orleans. He relinquished the School chairmanship in 2001 to accept the Jerome Goldman Endowed Academic Chair in Naval Architecture and Marine Engineering, which he holds presently. In 2006, he resumed duties as the Chairman of the UNO School of NAME, which is also his present position.

Nomenclature

$w(x,t), \dot{w}(x,t), \ddot{w}(x,t)$ vibration displacement, velocity, and acceleration, respectively

x,y,z,t   cartesian coordinates, time

E   Young's modulus

I   moment of inertia

c   hull beam damping coefficient

k   spring stiffness

μ hull beam mass distribution, including hydrodynamic added-mass

f   vibratory exciting force

ν viscoelastic modulus

DOF   degrees of freedom of discrete system model

N   number of total DOF, known+ unknown+ dynamic+static; propeller blade number

L   hull beam length; number of DOF unknown before solution

$L(r,\theta)$ lift distribution on propeller blades

M   number of dynamic DOF in discrete model; hull added mass; number of diesel engine cylinders

$M_{2\text{-}D}$ hull two-dimensional (2D) added mass

F   vibratory exciting force amplitude

W   vibratory displacement complex amplitude

W_c; W_s cosine and sine components of W

ω vibration frequency, in rad/sec

Ω_f characteristic rigid-body frequency

Ω_r characteristic flexural frequency

ζ_c hydrodynamic damping factor

ζ_v structural damping factor

κ modulus in beam vibration solution

ω_n resonant, or natural, frequency

$\omega_n{}^a$ anti-resonant frequency

$\Psi_n(x)$ mode shape vector for n^{th} natural mode

A_n solution constants in eigenfunction solution

F_n n^{th} mode modal exciting force

K_n n^{th} mode modal stiffness

ζ_n n^{th} mode modal damping factor

ζ one DOF system damping factor

α_n n^{th} mode modal phase angle

i $\sqrt{-1}$

$[m]$ vibration model mass matrix

$[k]$ vibration model stiffness matrix

$[c]$ vibration model damping matrix

$[f]$ vibration model exciting force vector

β phase of exciting force components

$[D]$ vibration model dynamic matrix

$[D]^*$ vibration model dynamic matrix with zero damping

$P(\omega)$ characteristic polynomial for determining model ω_n; $\Psi_n(x)$

Re   real part of complex quantity

Im   imaginary part of complex quantity

r   radius from the center of the propeller hub; diesel engine crank radius

θ propeller position angle, + CCW from top-dead-center looking forward

$g(r, \theta, p)$ function for assembling propeller bearing forces.

$G(r, \theta, p)$ amplitude of $g(r, \theta, p)$

f_{ip} ith propeller bearing force or moment component; i = 1 ... 6

$\beta_G(r)$ propeller blade geometric pitch angle at r

Kp   propeller induced pressure coefficient

Kf, K_{Fp} propeller induced force coefficient

F_m amplitude of harmonically oscillating modal excitation force on the hull

$\dot{q}$ volume rate of oscillation of cavitation source

p(z)   bare hull oscillation induced pressure in propeller plane z

V_m bare hull or cavitation volume velocity oscillation

Ω propeller angular velocity

c   sonic velocity in water

n, p   blade order multiples

k_n acoustic wave number; $n\omega/c$

δ particle radial displacement on a spherical surface

ρ water density

v_r particle radial velocity

λ_n acoustic wave length

I sound intensity

SPL sound pressure level

W acoustic power

dB decibel, for sound scaling

X amplitude of vibration displacement response

Y amplitude base vibration displacement

N_{2v} critical rpm for 2-noded vertical bending vibration

Δ displaced mass

T_m mean draft

$m(x)$ hull hydrodynamic added mass

$m_{2\text{-}D}(x)$ hull 2D hydrodynamic added mass distribution

Jn Lewis-Factor for nth mode hull added mass calculation

Z Conformal transformation for Lewis-form hull section mapping

$C(x)$	2D added mass distribution	$V_{nq}(r)$	q^{th} harmonic of wake velocity normal to blade section at radius r
$B(x)$	hull section beam distribution	$\alpha_s(r)$	propeller blade skew angle at radius r
h	superstructure height above main deck	$\gamma_q(r)$	phase angle of wake normal velocity at radius r
fe	fixed base superstructure natural frequency	$\theta(r)$	blade position angle for maximum normal velocity at blade radius r mid-chord line
f_R	deckhouse rocking natural frequency		
J	deckhouse mass moment of inertia; propeller advance ratio	$L_q(r)$	radial distribution of unsteady blade lift
$\bar{r}$	deckhouse radius of gyration about the effective pin at main deck	$C_{Lq}(r)$	radial distribution of unsteady blade lift coefficient
m	deckhouse mass	$\ell(r)$	radial distribution of propeller blade expanded chord length
M_{y1}, M_{y2}	iesel engine 1st and 2nd order vertical exciting moments	$C_s(r, k^*)$	Sears Function for lift of 2D section in a sinusoidal gust
M_{z1}	diesel engine 1st order transverse exciting moment amplitude	k^*	reduced frequency of sinusoidal gust
ℓ	diesel engine connecting rod length	θ_e	projected semi-chord of propeller blade at radius r
ℓ_c	longitudinal distance between diesel engine cylinder axes	T	propeller thrust
k_m	diesel engine firing order	$\dot{\forall}$	blade cavitation volume velocity variation in time
$v_x(r, \theta)/U$	axial wake velocity in propeller plane	$\dot{\forall}_q$	q^{th} harmonic of blade cavitation volume velocity variation
$v_t(r, \theta)/U$	tangential wake velocity in propeller plane		
U	vessel speed	C^C_{3hm}	m^{th} blade-rate harmonic of vertical hull surface force due to blade cavitation
$C_{xq}(r)$	complex amplitude of qth axial wake velocity coefficient in the propeller plane	C^{NC}_{3hm}	m^{th} blade-rate harmonic of non-cavitating vertical hull surface force
$C_{tq}(r)$	complex amplitude of qth tangential wake velocity coefficient in the propeller plane	v^*_{30x}	axial velocity induced in propeller plane by unit downward motion of bare hull for C^{NC}_{3hm} calc
W_j	Simpson's weighting factors for wake integration	$v^*_{31\theta}$	tangential velocity induced in propeller plane by unit downward motion of bare for hull C^{NC}_{3hm} calc
$v_n(r, \theta)$	relative wake velocity normal to propeller blade section at r		
β_G	geometric pitch angle of propeller blade section at r	ϕ^*_{30}	velocity potential induced in propeller plane by unit downward of the bare hull for C^C_{3hm} calc
β	hydrodynamic advance angle of propeller blade section at r		
$V_a(r)$	axial advance velocity of propeller	b_0	design waterline offset in the vertical plane of the propeller disc
R	propeller tip radius		
Q	wake maximum harmonic order		

1

Introduction

1.1 General. Much was accomplished in the 1970s and 1980s in improving the technology for designing ships for avoidance of excessive vibration. Because of this, as well as because of the downturn in ship production in the West, research and development in ship vibration experienced hiatus in the 1990s. It will therefore be seen that many of the reference sources cited in the previous edition of this chapter are retained in this edition. This is partially a natural consequence of fundamentally important basic material that serves as building blocks and never changes. New material is inserted where appropriate, but engineering technology that matured in the late 1980s is still mostly very representative of the state-of-the-art of ship vibration.

An example of the capability for achievement of vibration control that emerged from the 1980s was the success of the European cruise ship development programs of the 1990s. Vibration avoidance is a crucial issue with cruise ships laden with sensitive customers. The success was achieved via innovation gained by:

1. Placing engine rooms out of the immediate stern region to improve stern lines for low wake gradients.
2. Employing electric drive with the electric motors in articulating podded-propulsors, thereby avoiding the wake of shaft and bearing "shadows" shed into the propeller disk from forward.

Such progress is gratifying, but in spite of the success, one of the design problems of all modern ships and boats remains: avoidance of objectionable elastic vibration of the hull structure and machinery in response to external or internal forces. Such vibration, if ignored, will certainly occur, causing discomfort to passengers, interfering with performance of crew duties, and damaging or adversely affecting the operation of mechanical and electrical equipment on board the vessel.

Since mechanical vibration can be defined generally as the oscillatory motion of rigid, as well as elastic, bodies, the subject of ship vibration is actually very broad in scope. In fact, the ship dynamics problems of primary interest to the naval architect, excluding maneuvering, all involve some form of vibration.

For convenience, the overall response of a vessel can be separated into two parts: one is the motion as a rigid body in response to a seaway and the other is the elastic or flexural response of the hull or other structure to external or internal forces. Rigid-body motions are considered under the general subject of sea keeping and are therefore not usually referred to as vibration. Flexural vibration can be excited in the form of vertical and horizontal bending, torsion, and axial modes of the elastic structure of the hull girder, as well as in

the form of local vibration of substructures and components. Such vibration that is excited by propellers is a particularly troublesome problem, and it will be the principal subject of this chapter. Flexural vibration can also be excited directly by forces internal to rotating machinery and by the external forces of sea waves encountered by a ship. Vibration excited by sea waves (referred to as springing and whipping) is considered under both motions in waves and strength, although many of the basic principles of hull vibration covered in this chapter are directly applicable.

Concern about propeller-induced ship vibration has existed since the marine screw propeller was first developed in the mid-19th century; the French textbook *Theorie du Navire* (Pollard & Dudebout, 1894) included a chapter on propeller-induced ship vibration. In the early days, the relatively few blades per propeller and the low propeller revolutions per minute (RPM) excited ships at low frequency in a characteristically beamlike hull flexure. The early analytical work, such as that by Schlick (1884–1911) and Krylov (1936), therefore concentrated on the application of beam theory in developing methods to help avoid propeller-induced hull vibration problems.

As ships evolved, the character of propeller-induced vibration became more complex and vibration trouble became more frequent. The greatest problems occurred in the modern generation of oceangoing merchant ships, due in large part to two aspects of design evolution that, aside from a consideration of vibration, qualify as technological advancements. These two aspects are the location of engine rooms and accommodations aft into the immediate vicinity of the propeller(s) and the increase in ship power. The increased use of diesel engines has also contributed to increased frequency of vibration but not to as great a degree. Ship vibration has become a greater problem in recent years because of tightening of standards of acceptable vibration. Most commercial ship specifications now establish criteria on acceptable vibration; compliance must be demonstrated by the measurement of vibration on the vessel builder's trials. Today, exhaustive studies, employing both experimental and analytical methods, are conducted during the design of almost all large ships in attempting to avoid vibration troubles.

The object of this chapter is to discuss the basic theory and the practical problems of flexural vibration of ships' hulls, and of their substructures and components, with particular attention to propeller-excited vibration. Machinery-excited vibration is covered to a lesser extent.

A working knowledge of ship vibration requires the reader to be reasonably well-versed in mathematics and engineering mechanics, as well as in a set of "tricks of the trade" with which naval architects, and engineers in general, usually feel more comfortable. However, a comprehensive knowledge of ship vibration theory is not necessarily required in order to work effectively with the subject at certain levels. Hence, this chapter has been organized with the intent that readers with different interests and backgrounds can find material to meet their needs.

Section 2, Theory and Concepts, provides depth in understanding the fundamental concepts of ship vibration as well as a foundation for further study of the techniques employed in vibration analysis. It is intended primarily for those whose theoretical tools are relatively close to the surface of their working knowledge.

The naval architect or shipyard engineer interested more in design methods can avoid some of the risk of becoming bogged down in theory by proceeding to Section 3, Analysis and Design. This section is self-contained but refers back to Section 2 for formulas developed there. It deals with practical solutions to potential vibration problems that should be addressed during the design stage.

The last section, Criteria, Measurements, and Post-Trial Corrections, provides material for establishing whether vibration characteristics of a completed ship are satisfactory and how to make corrections, if necessary. The ship owner or operator, typically not particularly interested in design procedures and not at all interested in vibration theory and concepts, may proceed directly to this section.

1.2 Basic Definitions. The following basic definitions are provided for the uninitiated. The definitions are loose and aimed at the context most needed and most often used in the theory of vibration of ships.

Vibration—Vibration is a relatively small amplitude oscillation about a rest position. Figure 1 depicts the variation in vibratory displacement with time.

Amplitude—For vibration of a fixed level of severity (steady-state periodic vibration), amplitude is the maximum repeating absolute value of the vibratory response (i.e., displacement, velocity, acceleration). Displacement amplitude for steady-state vibration is denoted as A in Fig. 1. For transient vibration, a time-dependent amplitude sometimes may be defined.

Cycle—One cycle of vibration is the time between successive repeating points (see Fig. 1). The time required for completion of one cycle is its period.

Frequency—Frequency is the number of vibration cycles executed per unit time; it is the inverse of the vibration period.

Natural frequency—A natural frequency is a frequency at which a system vibrates when stimulated impulsively from the rest position. The requirement for natural vibration is that the system possesses both mass and stiffness. For continuous mass and stiffness distributions, the system possesses an infinite number of natural frequencies, even though only a relatively small number are usually of practical significance. On impulsive stimulation from rest, the continuous system will vibrate at all of its natural frequencies, in superposition; the degree of vibration at any particular natural frequency will depend on the characteristics of the impulsive stimulus.

Mode—Each different natural frequency of a system defines a mode of system vibration. The modes are ordered numerically upward from the natural frequency with the lowest value.

Mode shape—A mode shape is a distribution of relative amplitude, or displacement shape, associated with each mode. Figure 2 depicts mode shapes typical of a ship hull girder. The three vertical plane mode shapes shown correspond to the first three vertical plane flexural bending modes; two lower modes (not shown), with mode shapes corresponding to rigid-body heave and pitch, occur at lower natural frequencies. The lower shape in Fig. 2 is the one-noded, first mode torsional mode shape.

Node—A node is a null point in a distribution of vibratory displacement, or in a mode shape. In general, the number of nodes in a mode shape increases with modal order (natural frequency). This is the case of the ship hull girder vibration depicted in Fig. 2; modes 2V, 3V, and 4V have successively higher natural frequencies.

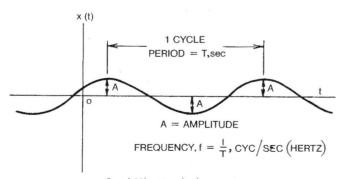

Fig. 1 Vibration displacement.

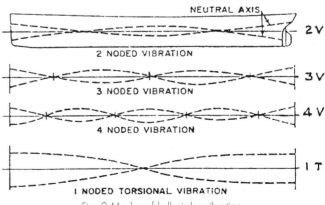

Fig. 2 Modes of hull girder vibration.

Excitation—Vibratory excitation is an applied time-dependent stimulus (force or displacement) that produces vibration. Excitation can be transient (e.g., impulsive), random, or periodic. A steady-state periodic excitation, such as approximately produced by a steadily operating ship propeller, produces a steady-state periodic forced vibration of the character of that depicted in Fig. 1.

Exciting frequency—For a steady-state periodic excitation, the exciting frequency is the number of cycles of the excitation completed per unit time, which is the inverse of the excitation period. Under steady-state conditions, the frequency of the vibration is always equal to the exciting frequency. However, the distribution of system vibration response at the steady-state exciting frequency can be viewed as a weighted superposition of the mode shapes of all the natural modes. The degree of participation of any mode is sensitive to the proximity of the natural frequency associated with that mode to the imposed exciting frequency.

Resonance—Resonance is the condition that occurs in steady-state forced vibration when the exciting frequency coincides with any one of the system natural frequencies. The common frequency is then also called a *resonant frequency*. At resonance, the vibration amplitude is limited only by system damping, ignoring

nonlinearities. The damping in engineering structures, including ships, is generally very light, so that resonant vibratory amplitudes are often disproportionately large relative to nonresonant levels. With the disproportionate amplification of one system mode at resonance, the distribution of system resonant vibration will often correspond closely to the mode shape of the resonant mode.

Bandwidth—Bandwidth is a range, or band, of frequency where a vibration and/or noise is concentrated.

Beat—Beating is a characteristic of systems excited by two or more excitation frequencies, the values of which are similar and vary only over a small range or are only slightly different. The resulting response contains a low *beat frequency*. The value of the beat frequency varies, but its maximum value is equal to the bandwidth of the exciting frequency variation.

Octave band—One of the standard frequency bands in which vibration (and noise) signals are analyzed (filtered) and presented (see Section 2.2.4).

Decibel (dB)—A quantification of vibration level used primarily in acoustics; dB is defined as 10 times the $\log_{10}$ of a vibration amplitude divided by a reference vibration amplitude (see Section 2.2.4).

Sound pressure level (SPL)—is defined as 20 times the $\log_{10}$ of an absolute value of the sound pressure divided by a reference sound pressure (see Section 2.2.4).

2
Theory and Concepts

2.1 Continuous Analysis. All systems that are capable of vibrating, including ships, have at least *piecewise* continuous properties. That is, the mass, elasticity, damping, and excitation properties are continuous within *pieces*, but may have jumps in value where the pieces connect. Unfortunately, mathematical models of piece-wise continuous systems that are at all general are of little use in vibration analysis because of the intractability of their solutions; discrete models are necessary for most practical purposes, as is shown in Section 2.2.

However, simple continuous models, representing idealizations of real systems, are extremely valuable in understanding basic vibration concepts. Their simple solutions can often provide surprising insight into the behavior of the complex systems whose basic character they approximate.

The simple continuous model that has been used repeatedly over the years to demonstrate certain fundamental aspects of ship vibration (Kennard, 1955; Todd, 1961) is the uniform continuous beam model of the ship hull. This model is depicted in Fig. 3 for the case of vertical vibration.

Here, the ship hull girder is represented by a uniform one-dimensional beam. The beam is supported by a uniform elastic foundation, of stiffness k per unit length,

representing the buoyancy spring of the water (water specific weight times section beam). The foundation has a uniformly distributed damping coefficient, c, representing hydrodynamic damping.

The uniform beam mass per unit length is μ (including hydrodynamic added mass), and its uniform stiffness is EI, where E is modulus of elasticity and I sectional moment of inertia. The beam is acted upon by the distributed forcing function, $f(x,t)$, which for purposes of example, represents the vibratory excitation due to the unsteady pressure field of a propeller.

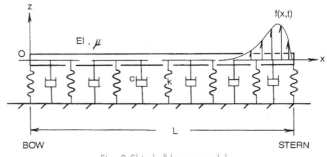

Fig. 3 Ship hull beam model.

The Fig. 3 model is, in a strict sense, a valid demonstration tool for propeller-induced ship vibration occurring typically at relatively low propeller RPM. At higher exciting frequencies associated with modern ship propellers operating near design RPM, the dynamics of mass systems sprung (i.e., connected by a structure that acts as a spring) from the hull girder, deckhouses for example, become important. However, as the vibration of the basic hull girder retains at least a beamlike character at high frequency, the Fig. 3 model is still instructive, although incomplete.

The differential equation of motion governing vibration of the Fig. 3 model is available from almost any general reference on mechanical vibration. Denoting $w(x,t)$ as the vertical vibratory displacement of the beam, the governing equation is

$$EI\frac{\partial^4 w}{\partial x^4} + vI\frac{\partial^5 w}{\partial x^4 \partial t} + \mu\frac{\partial^2 w}{\partial t^2}$$
$$+ c\frac{\partial w}{\partial t} + kw = f(x,t) \tag{1}$$

Aside from the second term on the left side, equation (1) represents the standard *Euler beam* on an elastic foundation. The second term in equation (1) derives from the inclusion of a viscoelastic term in the stress-strain law for the beam material (Kennard, 1955), v is the viscoelastic constant. The second term in equation (1), as well as the fourth, involves the first-time derivative of the displacement, and therefore represents damping; c is the hydrodynamic damping coefficient of the elastic foundation, by previous definition; vI in the second term in equation (1) represents a material damping coefficient of the hull beam.

The Euler beam representation, equation (1), can be easily extended to the *Timoshenko beam* by including beam rotational inertia and shear flexibility in the derivation. However, the additional terms introduced add substantial complexity to the equation as well as to the complexity of its possible analytic solutions. Since the purpose of this section is only to establish concepts and the formulas to be derived are not intended for actual application, shear flexibility and rotational inertia in the equation of motion are not included.

End conditions on the equation of motion are required for uniqueness of its solution. The end conditions on equation (1), corresponding to zero end moment and shear, are

$$\frac{\partial^2 w}{\partial x^2} = \frac{\partial^3 w}{\partial x^3} = 0 \quad \text{at } x = 0 \quad \text{and} \quad x = L \tag{2}$$

2.1.1 Steady-State Response to Periodic Excitation. In propeller-induced ship vibration, the steady propeller excitation is, in reality, a random excitation that remains stationary while conditions are unchanged. However, it is approximately periodic with fundamental frequency equal to the propeller RPM times the number of blades. The excitation is therefore approximately expressible as a Fourier series in the time variable. With steady-state vibratory response to the periodic excitation being the interest, $w(x,t)$ is likewise expressible in a Fourier series.

The procedure for solving the equation of motion, equation (1), for the steady-state vibration response is to substitute the two Fourier series representations for $w(x,t)$ and $f(x,t)$ into the equation. The time dependency is then cancelled out, and the resultant series of ordinary differential equations in x are solved term by term for the unknown coefficients of the displacement series.

For demonstration purposes, assume a one-term Fourier series (i.e., simple harmonic) representation for the excitation force distribution in time. Then optional forms are

$$f(x,t) = F(x)\cos(\omega t - \alpha) \tag{3}$$
$$= \text{Re } F(x)e^{i\omega t} \tag{4}$$

where, by identity

$$e^{i\omega t} \equiv \cos\omega t + i\sin\omega t$$

and Re denotes "real part of." $F(x)$ is the amplitude distribution of the excitation force along the length of the ship, and ω is its frequency. Defining ω as *blade-rate* frequency, $N\Omega$, where Ω is the propeller angular velocity and N the number of blades, equation (3) would be a valid approximation of $f(x,t)$ provided that the *fundamental harmonic* of the excitation is dominant (i.e., provided that the excitation at multiples of blade-rate frequency is relatively insignificant). This is often true, particularly in cases in which propeller blade cavitation does not occur.

For steady-state vibration in response to $f(x,t)$, $w(x,t)$ will have the similar form

$$w(x,t) = W_c(x)\cos\omega t + W_s(x)\sin\omega t$$
$$= \text{Re } W(x)e^{i\omega t} \tag{5}$$

where, in view of equation (5),

$$W(x) = W_c(x) - iW_s(x) \tag{6}$$

$W(x)$ is the unknown *complex* amplitude, which includes phase as well as amplitude information. $W(x)$ is to be determined by solution of the equation of motion.

Substitution of equations (4) and (6) into equation (1) and end conditions, equation (2), with cancellation of the time dependency, produces

$$EI\left(1 + i\frac{\omega v}{E}\right)\frac{d^4 W}{dx^4} - (\omega^2\mu - i\omega c - k)W = F(x) \tag{7}$$

with

$$\frac{d^2 W}{dx^2} = \frac{d^3 W}{dx^3} = 0 \quad \text{at } x = 0 \quad \text{and} \quad L \tag{8}$$

It is convenient to nondimensionalize the variables in equations (7) and (8) before considering solutions for $W(x)$. Redefine the variables in nondimensional form as

$$W = \frac{W}{L}, \quad x = \frac{x}{L}, \quad F = \frac{F}{EI/L^3}$$

Also define

$$\kappa^4 = \left(\frac{\omega}{\Omega_f}\right)^2 - 2i\zeta_c\left(\frac{\omega}{\Omega_f}\right) - \left(\frac{\Omega_r}{\Omega_f}\right)^2$$

wherein κ^4

$$\Omega_r = \sqrt{\frac{kL}{\mu L}}$$

is a characteristic rigid-body frequency;

$$\Omega_f = \sqrt{\frac{EI/L^3}{\mu L}}$$

is a characteristic flexural frequency;

$$\zeta_c = \frac{c}{2\mu\Omega_f}$$

is a hydrodynamic damping factor, and denote

$$\zeta_V = \frac{v\Omega_f}{2E}$$

as a structural damping factor.

Equation (7) then becomes

$$\left(1 + 2i\zeta_v\frac{\omega}{\Omega_f}\right)\frac{d^4W}{dx^4} - \kappa^4 W = F(x) \quad (9)$$

This is the nondimensional equation for steady-state vibration amplitude in response to harmonic excitation. Its end conditions are

$$\frac{d^2W}{dx^2} = \frac{d^3W}{dx^3} = 0 \quad at \quad x = 0 \quad and \quad 1$$

2.1.2 Undamped End-Forced Solution-Demonstrations. The simplest meaningful solution of equation (9) is obtained by specializing $F(x)$ to be a concentrated end force and discarding the damping terms. This solution, obtained by direct inversion of the reduced equation is

$$W(x) = \frac{F}{2\kappa^3} \cdot \frac{1}{1 - \cosh\kappa\cos\kappa}$$
$$\cdot [(\sinh\kappa - \sin\kappa)(\cos\kappa x + \cosh\kappa x) \quad (10)$$
$$- (\cosh\kappa - \cos\kappa)(\sin\kappa x + \sinh\kappa x)]$$

Here, the force is concentrated at the stern, $x = 1$ (see Fig. 3). With zero damping, $W(x)$ is pure real and κ is given by

$$\kappa^4 = (\omega/\Omega_f)^2 - (\Omega_r/\Omega_f)^2 \quad (11)$$

The solution, equation (10), permits several relevant observations. These are developed as described later.

2.1.2.1 RESONANT FREQUENCIES—ADDED MASS AND BUOYANCY EFFECTS. The undamped solution, equation (10), implies infinite vibration amplitude at the values of ω which make $\cosh\kappa\cos\kappa$ equal to unity. These values of ω are therefore the system *resonant frequencies*, which are denoted as ω_n. Denoting $\kappa = \kappa_n$ at values of ω equal to ω_n, the resonant frequencies correspond to the infinity of roots of

$$\cosh\kappa_n\cos\kappa_n = 1 \quad (12)$$

where, from equation (11),

$$\kappa_n^4 = (\omega_n/\Omega_f)^2 - (\Omega_r/\Omega_f)^2 \quad (13)$$

The first root of equation (12) is $\kappa_0 = 0$. This implies, from equation (13), that

$$w_0 = \Omega_r = \sqrt{\frac{kL}{\mu L}}$$

This is just the rigid-body heave, or pitch, resonant frequency; the two are the same for a ship with uniform (or longitudinally symmetric) mass and buoyancy distributions. At the low frequency of the rigid-body resonance corresponding to κ_0, the mass distribution μ is frequency dependent due to the surface wave effects in the hydrodynamic component of μ. The frequency dependence of μ diminishes as the vibratory frequency increases. In reality, ship hydrodynamic added mass is essentially invariant with frequency at frequencies corresponding to the hull flexural modes.

The second root of equation (12) is $\kappa_1 = 4.73$, which corresponds to the first hull flexural mode. All subsequent κ_n are greater than κ_1. Therefore, assuming μ to be independent of frequency for $n \geq 1$, Ω_f and Ω_r are constants in equation (13), and the first flexural mode resonant frequency, and all of those above it, are directly available from equation (13) as

$$\omega_n = \Omega_f\sqrt{\kappa_n^4 + (\Omega_r/\Omega_f)^2}; \, n = 1,...,\infty \quad (14)$$

with κ_n determined from equation (12).

For ships, the ratio Ω_r/Ω_f is typically on the order of 1, and therefore much smaller than κ_n^4 in equation (14). This demonstrates the fact that the effect of buoyancy in stiffening a ship hull in vertical flexural vibration exists but is insignificant in normal circumstances. Discarding Ω_r/Ω_f in equation (14), the beam resonant frequencies are approximated by

$$\omega_n = \kappa_n^2\Omega_f = \kappa_n^2\sqrt{\frac{EI/L^3}{\mu L}}; \, n \geq 1 \quad (15)$$

Being typically negligible, the effects of buoyancy will be discarded in all subsequent considerations of flexural vibration; Ω_r will be deleted in the definition of κ so that the existence of nonzero rigid-body modes $(n = 0)$ is ignored. Furthermore, Ω_f appearing in κ will be taken as frequency independent, since the hydrodynamic added mass in Ω_f is a constant at high frequency.

Note that although in the case of wave-excited vibration both rigid-body and flexural vibration occur, the two responses are essentially independent superpositions.

2.1.2.2 STERN VIBRATION LEVEL. Consider the vibration at the position of the concentrated excitation force by setting $x = 1$ in equation (10)

$$\frac{W(1)}{F} = \frac{\sinh\kappa\,\cos\kappa - \cosh\kappa\,\sin\kappa}{\kappa^3\,(1 - \cosh\kappa\,\cos\kappa)} \qquad (16)$$

For exciting frequencies in the range of the beam flexural resonant frequencies, the corresponding values of κ, as arguments of the hyperbolic functions, can be considered as large. That is, for large κ

$$\sinh\kappa \approx \cosh\kappa \approx \frac{1}{2}e^{\kappa}$$

Therefore, at high frequency

$$\frac{W(1)}{F} \approx \frac{\cos\kappa - \sin\kappa}{\kappa^3\,(2e^{-\kappa} - \cos\kappa)} \approx \frac{1}{\kappa^3}(\tan\kappa - 1) \qquad (17)$$

Equation (17) implies that, for a forcing function of fixed amplitude, the end vibration generally decreases with frequency as κ^{-3}, or $\omega^{-3/2}$. Zero vibration at the stern occurs at the *antiresonant frequencies*, $\omega_n{}^a$, corresponding approximately to

$$\tan\kappa_n{}^a = 1$$

or, from equation (15),

$$\omega_n{}^a/\Omega_f = [(4n + 1)\pi/4]^2; \quad n = 1, \ldots, \infty \qquad (18)$$

Large vibration occurs only in the immediate vicinity of the resonant frequencies, the flexural values of which, from equation (17), correspond approximately to

$$\tan\kappa_n = \pm\infty$$

or

$$\omega_n/\Omega_f = [(2n + 1)\pi/2]^2; \quad n = 1, \ldots, \infty \qquad (19)$$

As ω increases, equation (17) implies a limiting state where the vibration is zero except at the resonances. But the resonant frequencies, equation (19), at which the vibration is infinite, occur in the limit of large n, infinitely far apart.

The trend toward this limiting case is exhibited in Fig. 4, which is a plot of equation (17) in the frequency range of the first few flexural modes.

With regard to the relationship of equation (17) to actual ship vibration, it is not true, in general, that the spacing of the hull girder resonances increases as frequency increases. The disagreement is due to the exclusion of shear and rotational inertia in the beam model, as well as to the exclusion of the effects of local vibratory subsystems sprung from the hull beam. These ef-

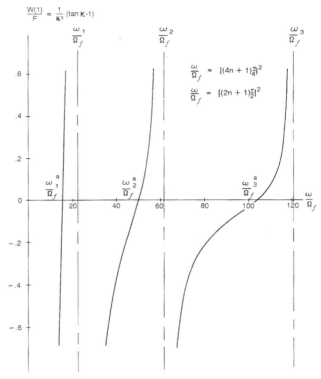

Fig. 4 Hull beam response characteristics.

fects become influential in ship hull girder vibration at high frequency.

The vibration is also, in reality, certainly not infinite at the resonant frequencies; this prediction is due to the deletion of damping in the solution to equation (9).

It is likewise not true that propeller-induced vibration has a generally decreasing trend with frequency, as equation (17) implies. In reality, however, the amplitude of the propeller excitation, in this case F, increases with frequency, roughly as frequency squared. With an ω^2 variation of F in equation (17), $W(1)$ then increases generally as $\omega^{1/2}$, which is more realistic than decreasing as $\omega^{-3/2}$.

2.1.2.3 RELATIVE VIBRATION OF BOW AND STERN. Setting $x = 0$ in equation (10), the vibration amplitude at the beam end opposite that to which the excitation is applied is

$$\frac{W(0)}{F} = \frac{\sinh\kappa - \sin\kappa}{\kappa^3\,(1 - \cosh\kappa\,\cos\kappa)} \qquad (20)$$

Using equations (16) and (20), the ratio of the end displacements is

$$\frac{W(0)}{W(1)} = \frac{\sinh\kappa - \sin\kappa}{\sinh\kappa\,\cos\kappa - \cosh\kappa\,\sin\kappa} \qquad (21)$$

Again, replacing the hyperbolic functions by the exponential for large κ

$$\frac{W(0)}{W(1)} = \frac{1 - 2\sin\kappa\, e^{-\kappa}}{\cos\kappa - \sin\kappa} \cong \frac{1}{\cos\kappa - \sin\kappa}$$

$$= \frac{1}{\sqrt{2}\,\cos(\kappa + \pi/4)} \qquad (22)$$

At the antiresonant frequencies, equation (18), $W(0)/W(1)$ becomes infinite since $W(1) = 0$ by definition of the antiresonance. At the resonant frequencies, equation (19), $W(0)/W(1) = \pm1$, by equation (12). The minimum absolute value of the displacement ratio occurs at $\cos(\kappa + \pi/4) = \pm1$. Its value is

$$\min|W(0)/W(1)| = 1/\sqrt{2}$$

The frequencies at which this minimum value occurs are

$$\frac{\omega}{\Omega_f} = [(4n+3)\pi/4]^2; \quad n = 1,\ldots,\infty \qquad (23)$$

This prediction is definitely contradictory to observations of ship vibration at high frequency. The simple undamped end-forced solution predicts that the vibration level at the ship bow should never be less than roughly 70% of the vibration at the stern. In reality, propeller-induced ship hull girder vibration is known to concentrate at the stern at high propeller RPM, with the vibration diminishing rapidly forward and often being hardly detectable in the vessel forebody.

A reconciliation of theory and observation as to this particular point requires a more general solution to equation (9), which includes damping as well as a less restricted characterization of the propeller excitation. However, the direct analytic solution procedure used to produce equation (10) is no longer suitable for providing the desired insight in the more general case.

2.1.3 A More General Solution: Modal Expansion. The modal, or *eigenfunction*, expansion technique allows damping as well as an arbitrary excitation character to be handled with relative ease. Basically, modal expansion is an expression of the fact that the vibration can be viewed as a superposition of the independent natural modes. The solution to the equation of motion is expressed as an infinite series, versus the alternative closed-form possibility represented by equation (10). The series is expanded in terms of the infinite set of normal modes of the unforced, undamped system.

2.1.3.1 NATURAL FREQUENCIES AND MODE SHAPES. Returning to the equation of motion for the Fig. 3 uniform beam, equation (9), the unforced, undamped system in this case corresponds to equation (9) with zero damping and excitation

$$\frac{d^4W}{dx^4} - \kappa^4 W = 0 \qquad (24)$$

$$\frac{d^2W}{dx^2} = \frac{d^3W}{dx^3} = 0 \quad at \quad x = 0 \ and \ 1$$

where κ is defined by equation (11). The solution to the homogeneous differential equation, equation (24), is, for $\kappa \neq 0$

$$W(x) = C_1 \sin\kappa\, x + C_2 \cos\kappa\, x$$
$$+ C_3 \sinh\kappa\, x + C_4 \cosh\kappa\, x \qquad (25)$$

Applying the two end conditions at $x = 0$ eliminates two of the four constants in equation (25) as

$$C_2 = C_4, \quad C_1 = C_3 \qquad (26)$$

Application of the remaining end conditions at $x = 1$ gives the following simultaneous equations for determining C_3 and C_4

$$\begin{bmatrix} \sin\kappa - \sinh\kappa & \cos\kappa - \cosh\kappa \\ \cos\kappa - \cosh\kappa & -\sin\kappa - \sinh\kappa \end{bmatrix} \begin{vmatrix} C_3 \\ C_4 \end{vmatrix} = \begin{vmatrix} 0 \\ 0 \end{vmatrix} \qquad (27)$$

or

$$[B]|C| = |0|$$

Then, by inversion

$$|C| = [B]^{-1}|0|$$

Therefore, unless $[B]$ is singular, the only solution to equations (27) is $|C| = |0|$. But this implies that $W(x) = 0$, which is not of interest. Nonzero $|C|$ and nonzero $W(x)$ therefore require that $[B]$ be singular. $[B]$ is singular only if its determinant is zero. From equations (27),

$$\det[B] = -2(1 - \cos\kappa \cosh\kappa) \qquad (28)$$

denote the values of κ which make $\det[B] = 0$ as κ_n; these values are the system eigenvalues. The infinite set of eigenvalues is determined so that equation (28) is zero, so that

$$\cos\kappa_n \cosh\kappa_n = 1, \quad n = 1, \ldots, \infty \qquad (29)$$

But this is just equation (12), which established the system resonant frequencies. From equation (11), ignoring the Ω_r term,

$$\kappa_n^4 = (\omega_n/\Omega_f)^2 \qquad (30)$$

where ω_n was identified as the *resonant* frequencies. But under present considerations, ω_n are the frequencies corresponding to unforced and undamped, or *natural*, system vibration; the system resonant frequencies are therefore synonymous with the system natural frequencies.

Nonzero values of C_3 and C_4 from equations (27) therefore exist only at values of ω, satisfying equation (29). However, the values of the constants, while not zero, are indeterminate, since the coefficient determinant is zero at these frequencies. The fact that the determinant of the coefficients is zero at the natural frequencies implies that the two equations (27) are linearly dependent at the natural frequencies. That is, two independent equations from which to determine the two constants are not available. The only information available from equations (27) is the relationship between C_3 and C_4 at the natural frequencies. Either one of the two equations can be used for this purpose; the same result will be obtained because of the linear dependency. From the second equation of equation (27)

$$\frac{C_3}{C_4} = \frac{\sin\kappa_n + \sinh\kappa_n}{\cos\kappa_n - \cosh\kappa_n} \tag{31}$$

Substitution of equation (31) and equation (26) back into the homogeneous solution equation (25) gives the beam vibration amplitude at the natural frequencies, as a function of x, except for a constant factor. This *relative* amplitude distribution at the natural frequencies is the eigenfunction, or mode shape, and is denoted by ψ_n. From equation (25), the mode shape for the Fig. 3 beam is

$$\psi_n(x) = C_4 \left[\cos\kappa_n x + \cosh\kappa_n x + \right.$$

$$\left. + \frac{\sin\kappa_n + \sinh\kappa_n}{\cos\kappa_n - \cosh\kappa_n}(\sin\kappa_n x + \sinh\kappa_n x)\right] \tag{32}$$

The constant C_4 is arbitrary and is conventionally set to unity.

Equation (32) is the beam mode shape for $\kappa \neq 0$. This function has the character of the vertical mode shapes depicted in Fig. 2 of Section 1.2; increasing n corresponds to increasing node number.

For $\kappa = 0$, the solution to the homogeneous system, equation (24) is

$$W(x) = C_1 + C_2 x + C_3 x^2 + C_4 x^3 \tag{33}$$

The end conditions at $x = 0$ reduce equation (33) to

$$W(x) = C_1 + C_2 x \tag{34}$$

which satisfies the end conditions at $x = 1$ identically. The mode shape identified with equation (34) is therefore the zeroth order rigid-body heave/pitch mode, the corresponding natural frequency of which was previously identified as Ω_r by equations (12) and (13); Ω_r has been assumed to be zero in consideration of the flexural modes.

2.1.3.2 VIBRATORY DISPLACEMENT. Modal expansion expresses the solution of the equations of motion, equation (9), as a weighted summation of the infinite set of mode shapes

$$W(x) = \sum_{n=1}^{\infty} A_n \psi_n(x) \tag{35}$$

Back substituting equation (35) into equation (9) and utilizing the *orthogonality* property of the mode shapes, which uncouples the A_n terms in equation (35) (see Section 2.2, equation (72), and the material immediately following), the A_n terms are determined as

$$A_n = \frac{F_n / K_n}{1 - (\omega/\omega_n)^2 + 2i\zeta_n\omega/\omega_n} \tag{36}$$

In equation (36), F_n, K_n, and ζ_n represent the following.
Modal exciting force:

$$F_n = \int_{x=0}^{1} F(x)\psi_n(x)dx \tag{37}$$

Modal stiffness:

$$K_n = \left(\frac{\omega_n}{\Omega_f}\right)^2 \int_{x=0}^{1} \Psi_n^{\,2}(x)dx \tag{38}$$

Modal damping factor:

$$\zeta_n = \zeta_v(\omega_n/\Omega_f) + \zeta_c(\Omega_f/\omega_n) \tag{39}$$

Substitution of equation (36) into equation (35) gives the complex vibration amplitude

$$W(x) = \sum_{n=1}^{\infty}\left[\frac{F_n/K_n}{1 - (\omega/\omega_n)^2 + 2i\zeta_n\omega/\omega_n}\right]\psi_n(x) \tag{40}$$

Substitution of this result into equation (5), and using a trigonometric identity, gives the vibration displacement at any point x along the beam at any time

$$w(x,t) = \sum_{n=1}^{\infty}\cdot\left[\frac{F_n/K_n}{\sqrt{\left(1-(\omega/\omega_n)^2\right)^2 + \left(2\zeta_n\omega/\omega_n\right)^2}}\right]\psi_n(x)\cos(\omega t - \alpha_n) \tag{41}$$

The modal phase angle, α_n, relative to F_n, is

$$\alpha_n = \tan^{-1}\left[\frac{2\zeta_n\omega/\omega_n}{1 - (\omega/\omega_n)^2}\right]$$

The form of equation (41) demonstrates that modal expansion can be viewed as just a superposition of the independent responses of an infinite number of equivalent one-degree-of-freedom systems. The stiffness, damping, and excitation of each equivalent system are the modal values corresponding to equations (37), (38), and (39). The equivalent mass would be the modal mass, $M_n = K_n/\omega_n^2$. The response of each of the one-degree-of-freedom systems is distributed according to the mode shapes of the respective modes.

2.1.3.3 RELATIVE VIBRATION OF BOW AND STERN. The reasons for the rapid attenuation of hull girder vibration on moving forward from the stern, which were left unexplained by the simple theory of the last section, can now be reconsidered with the aid of the modal expansion, equation (40).

It is first convenient, although not at all necessary, to *normalize* the eigenfunction set, equation (32), by assigning specific values to the constant C_4. Choosing a value of unity of the $\psi_n(x)$ at the forcing end

$$\psi_n(1) = 1; \quad n = 1, \ldots, \infty \tag{42}$$

C_4 in equation (32) is evaluated as

$$C_4 = \frac{\cos\kappa_n - \cosh\kappa_n}{2\sin\kappa_n \sinh\kappa_n} \tag{43}$$

Then from equations (43) and (32), the eigenfunction at $x = 0$ has the values

$$\psi_n(0) = (-1)^{n+1}; \quad n = 1, \ldots, \infty \tag{44}$$

It will also be notationally convenient to define, $W_n(x) \equiv A_n\psi_n(x)$ where A_n is given by equation (36). Equation (40) is then, alternatively

$$W(x) = \sum_{n=1}^{\infty} W_n(x) \tag{45}$$

By equations (42), (44), and (45), the displacements at the two ends of the beam are

$$W(1) = \sum_{n=1}^{\infty} W_n(1)$$

and

$$\tag{46}$$

$$W(0) = \sum_{n=1}^{\infty} (-1)^{n+1} W_n(1)$$

Equation (46) shows that the absolute values of the displacement components from each mode are the same at the beam ends. Differences in the sums must therefore be due only to the alternating form of the series for $W(0)$, associated with phase changes occurring within the displacement components at the forcing end. In fact, this character of the displacement series, equation (46), is the basis for understanding the reasons for the rapid decay of hull girder vibration forward from the stern. Figure 5 is intended as an aid in this purpose. Figure 5 is composed of sketches of the W_n components for six modes, arbitrarily, and their summations, for three different cases.

The left column in Fig. 5 depicts the displacement for the undamped beam with the concentrated force applied at the extreme end. This was the case studied in the last section and for which the minimum ratio of end displacements was predicted to be never less than $1/\sqrt{2}$. The center column in Fig. 5 represents the case in which damping remains zero but the concentrated force is applied at a position $x = x_0$ slightly less than 1, corresponding to a typical propeller position. In the third column on Fig. 5, the force has been replaced at the beam end but damping has been assumed to be nonzero and significant.

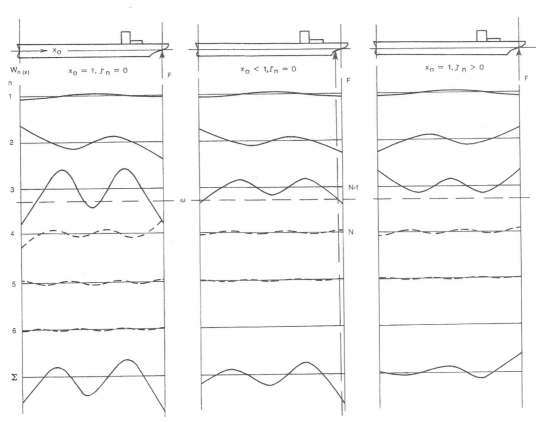

Fig. 5 Hull beam response characteristics.

The exciting frequency is assumed to lie arbitrarily between modes 3 and 4 in Fig. 5. The value of ω can be considered as that given by equation (23) with $n = 4$; equation (23) predicts the frequencies at which min $|W(0)/W(1)| = 1/\sqrt{2}$ occurs for the undamped, end-forced case. Consider the three cases of Fig. 5 individually.

Case 1—Undamped, end forced. From equation (40), with $x_0 = 1$ and for $\zeta_n = 0$

$$W_n(x) = \frac{F/K_n}{1 - (\omega/\omega_n)^2} \psi_n(x) \qquad (47)$$

In general, the modal forces for the three cases of Fig. 5 are $F_n = F\psi_n(x_0)$, by equation (37). For $x_0 = 1$ in the first case, $F_n = F$ for all n since $\psi_n(1) = 1$ by equation (42). For ω between the two resonant frequencies, ω_{N-1} and ω_N, the beam end displacements can be written from equations (46) and (47) as

$$W(1) = -\sum_{n=1}^{N-1} |W_n(1)| + \sum_{n=N}^{\infty} |W_n(1)|$$

$$W(0) = -\sum_{n=1}^{N-1} (-1)^{n+1} |W_n(1)|$$
$$+ \sum_{n=N}^{\infty} (-1)^{n+1} |W_n(1)| \qquad (48)$$

Here, the sign change occurring in the denominator of equation (47) at $n = N$ has been explicitly assigned. At the end $x = 1$, all of the modes below ω are of the same sign, but of opposite sign to the modes above ω. Imperfect cancellation occurs, with the lower modes dominating the upper. At $x = 0$, on the other hand, interferences occur among the groups of modes both below and above ω due to the alternating signs shown in equation (48). The dominant terms immediately above and below ω, that is, $W_{n-1}(0)$ and $W_n(0)$, have the same signs, however, and support rather than cancel. As a result, $W(0)$ is relatively large. In fact, the ratio $|W(0)/W(1)| = 1/\sqrt{2}$ occurring at ω for $x_0 = 1$ and $\zeta_n = 0$ is a maximum value of the minimum ratio. This is because both repositioning the excitation force forward and allowing nonzero damping result in a more rapid attenuation of displacement away from the forcing point.

Case 2—Undamped, $x_0 < 1$. Considering the case where $x_0 < 1$, which corresponds to the center column in Fig. 5, the modal force is

$$F_n = F\psi_n(x_0)$$

in equation (40). The modal forces now converge with increasing n, since, as the aftermost beam nodal point moves aft toward the forcing point with increasing n, the $\psi_n(x_0)$ values decrease. Thus, the higher modes become *less excitable* by the concentrated force. The result is a decrease in the cancellation in $W(1)$, by equation (48), as the net displacement produced by the modes above ω decreases relative to the net contribution from below.

Also, a weakening of the modes above ω reduces the support of the large N^{th} mode in $W(0)$, relative to the $(N - 1)^{\text{th}}$. This results in a relative decrease in $W(0)$, with respect to $W(1)$, and a larger difference in the end displacements. This decreasing propeller excitability of the higher hull girder modes by virtue of convergence of the modal force series was the explanation given by Baier and Ormondroyd (1952) for the rapid attenuation of propeller-induced hull girder vibration forward from the stern region.

Case 3—Damped, end-forced. Turning to the case of nonzero damping, but with $F_n = F$, the terms in the displacement series are

$$W_n(x) = \frac{F/K_n}{1 - (\omega/\omega_n)^2 + 2i\zeta_n\omega/\omega_n} \psi_n(x) \qquad (49)$$

If the modal damping factor, ζ_n, in equation (49) increases with n, then the convergence of the displacement series is accelerated, with the same effects as produced by convergence of the modal forces just considered.

Damping also modifies the relative phases of the modes. This occurs most strongly for modes in the immediate vicinity of the exciting frequency, since the damping in the denominator of equation (49) is relatively strongest for ω/ω_n in the vicinity of 1. For zero damping, the modes below the exciting frequency are 180 degrees out of phase with the modes above due to the sign change in the denominator of equation (47). Damping spreads the phase shift. If the damping is strong enough, the most dominant modes to either side of the exciting frequency can be approximately in phase and 90 degrees out of phase with the exciting force. This is the situation depicted in Fig. 5, where damping has delayed the phase shift in the two modes below ω. The result is increasing modal interference with distance away from the forcing point.

The effect depicted in the left column of Fig. 5 is contingent upon a modal damping factor that increases with modal order and/or is relatively large in the modes in the vicinity of the exciting frequency. In this regard, reconsider the modal damping factor that arose in the derivation of the uniform beam modal expansion, equation (39)

$$\zeta_n = \zeta_v(\omega_n/\Omega_f) + \zeta_c(\Omega_f/\omega_n)$$

The structural damping factor, ζ_v, is a constant, by equation (9). The hydrodynamic damping factor, ζ_c, has not been specifically defined, but it actually has a decreasing magnitude with frequency. Furthermore, ω_n/Ω_f is large for all n. Therefore, for n large

$$\zeta_n \cong \zeta_v(\omega_n/\Omega_f) = (v/2E)\omega_n$$

ζ_n, therefore, increases with n, and becomes large at large n corresponding to ω at high frequency excitation. The ζ_n developed with the idealized beam model therefore appears to meet the requirements for the effects of damping exhibited in Fig. 5. Kennard (1955) suggested high hull damping in the frequency range of propeller excitation for the concentration of vibration in the stern of vessels when operating at high propeller RPM.

This discussion with regard to Fig. 5 should help to avoid the common misconception that the concentration of propeller-induced vibration in the stern of a vessel is evidence that the vessel is exhibiting something other than beamlike vibration. To the contrary, sternward concentration of vibration at high frequency is due to interference in the beam modes at the bow and support at the stern. As shown, this occurrence is due both to increasing modal damping and decreasing modal excitability as modal order, and exciting frequency, increase.

2.2 Discrete Analysis

2.2.1 Mathematical Models. Modern day ship vibration analysis almost exclusively employs mathematical models that are nonuniform and discrete, rather than uniform and continuous. Such models represent the continuous mass, stiffness, damping, and excitation characteristics of the physical structure at a discrete number of points, which are called *nodal points.*

The equivalent nodal point properties are translated in terms of an assemblage of discrete, or *finite,* elements; the finite elements interconnect the nodal points of the structural model. (Note that these nodal points are not the same as the nodes defined in Section 1.2.)

In analyzing the discrete model, all forces and displacements are referred to the model nodal points. In general, six components of displacement, consisting of three translations and three rotations, and six corresponding components of force can exist at each nodal point of the model. The model is usually constrained, however, so that fewer than the possible six displacements are allowed at any nodal point. The number of such displacements allowed at any point is referred to as its *degrees of freedom.* If mass, or mass moment of inertia, is associated with a particular nodal point displacement, then that displacement defines a *dynamic* degree of freedom. Otherwise, the degree of freedom is *static.* While the total number of degrees of freedom of continuous systems is always infinite, the total number of degrees of freedom of a discrete model is finite, being the sum of the numbers assigned to each of the model nodal points.

Discrete analysis of ship vibration can be performed to any arbitrary level of detail, with model complexity limited primarily by available computing facilities. Often, the ship hull girder, as considered in the last section, is modeled along with its sprung substructures—deckhouses, decks, double-bottoms, etc.—in a single discrete model (Kagawa, 1978; Reed, 1971; Sellars & Kline, 1967).

In many cases, meaningful estimates of substructure vibration characteristics can also be obtained using only a discrete model of the substructure, with approximate boundary conditions applied at its attachment to the hull girder (Sandstrom & Smith, 1979).

Discrete analysis is conveniently demonstrated by an idealized example of the latter approach noted above. Consider the simple finite element model for a ship deckhouse shown in Fig. 6. Here, the house is modeled two-dimensionally as a rigid box of mass m and radius of gyration $\bar{r}$.

The house front is taken, typically, as a continuation of the forward engine room bulkhead; the connection at main deck is assumed to act as a simple pin allowing completely free rotation. The parallel connection of finite elements with axial stiffness and axial damping represents the supporting structure along the house after bulkhead. This structure would be composed, typically, of pillars erected within the engine room cavity. The house is base excited by the vertical vibratory displacement of the hull girder, $w(\xi, t)$, ξ now being the axial coordinate along the hull girder. The applied base displacements, $w(\xi_1, t)$ and $w(\xi_2, t)$, are the hull girder displacements at the forward engine room bulkhead and at the base of the after foundation; $w(\xi_1, t)$ and $w(\xi_2, t)$ are assumed at this point to be specified independently in advance.

Use of the Fig. 6 model for serious vibration analysis is not entirely valid in two respects. Primarily, the typical deckhouse does not truly act as if rigid at propeller excitation frequencies. While the underdeck supporting structure is quite often the predominant flexibility in propeller-induced deckhouse vibration, the bending and shear flexibilities of the house itself can usually not be considered as unimportant. Some degree of interaction of the house with the hull girder also occurs. Because of this, the base displacements are not easily prescribed with accuracy independently. In spite of these shortcomings, the simple Fig. 6 deckhouse model is instructive; it captures the basic characteristics of fore- and aft-deckhouse vibration in the spirit of the simple uniform beam model for hull girder vertical vibration studied in the last section.

Proceeding as described, the degree-of-freedom assignments of the Fig. 6 finite element model are shown in Fig. 7. Here, x_j is used to denote generalized displacement (i.e., rotation or translation). In view of the assumed house rigidity, all displacements in the vertical/fore-and-aft plane can be specified in terms of the three assigned in Fig. 7. All other possible displacements at the two nodal points of the Fig. 7 model are assigned zero values by virtue of their omission. Of the three total degrees of freedom assigned in Fig. 7, two are dynamic degrees of freedom. These are x_1 and x_2, as they are associated with the house mass moment of inertia and house mass, respectively. x_3 is a static degree of freedom.

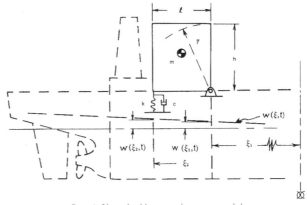

Fig. 6 Ship deckhouse vibration model.

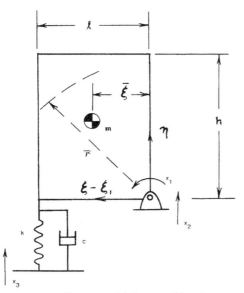

Fig. 7 Deckhouse model degrees of freedom.

Also, two of the three degrees of freedom are specified from Fig. 6 as

$$x_2 \equiv w(\xi_1, t) \quad \text{and} \quad x_3 \equiv w(\xi_2, t)$$

Once x_1 is determined, the vertical and fore-and-aft displacements at any point (ξ, η) on the house are available, respectively, as

$$w(\xi, \eta, t) = w(\xi_1, t) - x_1(t)(\xi - \xi_1)$$
$$u(\xi, \eta, t) = x_1(t)\eta \qquad (50)$$

2.2.2 Equations of Motion. The equations of motion governing the general finite element model are derived as follows.

It is first required that the model be in dynamic equilibrium in all of its degrees of freedom simultaneously. Application of Newton's Law in each degree of freedom, in turn, produces

$$[m]|\ddot{x}| = -|f_s| - |f_d| + |f| \qquad (51)$$

where, for M total degrees of freedom, $[m]$ is the $M \times M$ model mass matrix, $|\ddot{x}|$ is the $M \times 1$ nodal point acceleration vector, and $|f_s|$, $|f_d|$, and $|f|$ are the $M \times 1$ nodal point stiffness, damping, and excitation force vectors, respectively.

The characteristics of the model finite elements are established in advance to satisfy compatibility and material constitutive requirements on the local level. Satisfaction of these requirements for linear behavior leads to the following relations between the nodal point internal forces and the nodal point displacements

$$|f_s| = [k]|x| \qquad |f_d| = [c]|\dot{x}| \qquad (52)$$

Here, $[k]$ is the model stiffness matrix and $[c]$ is the model damping matrix, both of which are square matrices of order M.

Substitution of equation (52) into equation (51) produces the linear equations of motion governing the general discrete model

$$[m]|\ddot{x}| + [c]|\dot{x}| + [k]|x| = |f| \qquad (53)$$

This $M \times M$ system of equations can be readily solved for the unknown nodal point displacements once $[m]$, $[c]$, $[k]$, and $|f|$ are specified.

Actually, the equations of motion can be interpreted as a general statement and conveniently used to determine their own coefficients.

For example, if the accelerations and velocities are set to zero, equation (53) reduces to

$$[k]|x| = |f|$$

In expanded notation:

$$\begin{vmatrix} f_1 \\ f_2 \\ \cdot \\ \cdot \\ \cdot \\ f_M \end{vmatrix} = \begin{bmatrix} k_{11} & k_{12} & \cdots & k_{1M} \\ k_{21} & k_{22} & & \\ \cdot & & & \\ \cdot & & & \\ \cdot & & & \\ k_{M1} & \cdots & & k_{MM} \end{bmatrix} \begin{vmatrix} x_1 \\ x_2 \\ \cdot \\ \cdot \\ \cdot \\ x_M \end{vmatrix}$$

The subscripts refer to the numbers assigned to the nodal point degrees of freedom. Now, defining the k_{ij} requires, in addition to zero velocities and accelerations, that all displacements x_i be zero except for $i = j$, and set $x_j = 1$. Then, for any degree of freedom i, multiplication gives

$$f_i = k_{ij}$$

The k_{ij} is, therefore, defined as the force in degree of freedom i due to a unit displacement in degree of freedom j, with all other degrees of freedom completely restrained. Complete restraint means restraint from acceleration, velocity, and displacement.

Also, as to the matter of signs, the designation force in degree of freedom i is interpreted as the force required at i in order to accomplish the degree of freedom assignment at i.

The corresponding definitions of m_{ij} and c_{ij} are similarly derived from the general equation (53) by making the appropriate degree of freedom assignments. Definitions for m_{ij} and c_{ij} identical to that above for k_{ij} result, but with unit accelerations and velocities, respectively, replacing the unit displacements.

In calculating the components of the excitation force vector, f_i, the model is completely restrained in all degrees of freedom. f_i is then the resultant of the applied forces tending to overcome the restraint in degree of freedom i.

In this connection consider again the simple model of Fig. 7. The displacements in the three degrees of freedom are x_1, x_2, and x_3, with x_1 to be determined and the other two specified. By applying zero and unit accelerations, velocities, and displacements in the three degrees of freedom, in turn, the mass, damping, stiffness, and excitation force matrices are assembled by the rules stated above as

$$[m]=\begin{bmatrix} m\bar{r}^2 & -m\bar{\xi} & 0 \\ -m\bar{\xi} & m & 0 \\ 0 & 0 & 0 \end{bmatrix}$$

$$[c]=\begin{bmatrix} c\ell^2 & -c\ell & c\ell \\ -c\ell & c & -c \\ c\ell & -c & c \end{bmatrix}$$

$$[k]=\begin{bmatrix} k\ell^2 & -k\ell & k\ell \\ -k\ell & k & -k \\ k\ell & -k & k \end{bmatrix}$$

$$|f|=\begin{vmatrix} 0 \\ f_2 \\ f_3 \end{vmatrix} \tag{54}$$

The force components f_2 and f_3 in the excitation force vector above are the unknown forces associated with the known displacements x_2 and x_3; f_1 is zero as no external moment is applied at the pin connection.

This example demonstrates the general case. Either the applied external force, f_i, or displacement, x_i, must be specified for each degree of freedom; both will never be known prior to solution of the system equations, but one of the two must be known. The equations corresponding to the known forces are first solved for the unknown displacements. The unknown forces are then calculated using the then completely known displacements, with the equations corresponding to the unknown forces. For the Fig. 7 system, the first part of the operation described above produces a single equation of motion for determining the single unknown displacement x_1. It is

$$m\bar{r}^2\,\ddot{x}_1 + c\ell^2\,\dot{x}_1 + k\ell^2\,x_1$$
$$= m\bar{\xi}\,\ddot{x}_2 + c\ell(\dot{x}_2 - \dot{x}_3) + k\ell(x_2 - x_3) \tag{55}$$

On solving this equation for x_1, the unknown force components, f_2 and f_3, are then determined from the two remaining equations by multiplication as

$$\begin{vmatrix} f2 \\ f3 \end{vmatrix}=\begin{bmatrix} -m\bar{\xi} & m & 0 \\ 0 & 0 & 0 \end{bmatrix}\begin{vmatrix} \ddot{x}_1 \\ \ddot{x}_2 \\ \ddot{x}_3 \end{vmatrix}$$
$$+\begin{bmatrix} -c\ell & c & -c \\ c\ell & -c & c \end{bmatrix}\begin{vmatrix} \dot{x}_1 \\ \dot{x}_2 \\ \dot{x}_3 \end{vmatrix}$$
$$+\begin{bmatrix} -k\ell & k & -k \\ k\ell & -k & k \end{bmatrix}\begin{vmatrix} x_1 \\ x_2 \\ x_3 \end{vmatrix} \tag{56}$$

2.2.3 Solutions. For L of the total M model nodal point displacements unknown, L governing differential equations, in the general form of equation (53), must be solved. The $L \times 1$ force vector in equation (53) will be completely known in terms of the L applied force components and the $M - L$ applied displacements.

The same basic solution procedure applied in the continuous analysis of the last section is also followed here. The approximate periodicity of the propeller excitation allows the time variable to be separated from the differential equations by the use of Fourier series. For propeller angular velocity Ω and blade number N, define $\omega \equiv mN\Omega$ as the mth harmonic propeller exciting frequency. Then, for $|F|$ and $|X|$ representing the mth harmonic complex force and displacement amplitude vectors, the equations of motion, equation (53), can be satisfied harmonic by harmonic by solving

$$\{-\omega^2[m] + i\omega[c] + [k]\}|X| = |F| \tag{57}$$

Define the system *dynamic matrix* as $[D]$

$$[D] = -\omega^2[m] + i\omega[c] + [k] \tag{58}$$

Equation (57) is then

$$[D]|X| = |F| \tag{59}$$

with solution

$$|X| = [D]^{-1}|F| \tag{60}$$

Returning to the deckhouse model in Figs. 6 and 7 with

$$|x| = \mathrm{Re}|X|e^{i\omega t}$$

the system dynamic matrix, from equation (55), is

$$[D] = -\omega^2 m\bar{r}^2 + i\omega c\ell^2 + k\ell^2 \tag{61}$$

which is a 1×1 matrix on the single unknown complex amplitude, X_1. Likewise, the complex exciting force vector in equation (55) is

$$|F| \equiv F_1 = -\omega^2 m\bar{\xi}X_2 + (i\omega c\ell + k\ell)(X_2 - X_3)$$

The inversion required by equation (60), using equation (61), is then simply

$$X_1 = \frac{-\omega^2 m\bar{\xi}X_2 + (i\omega c\ell + k\ell)(X_2 - X_3)}{-\omega^2 m\bar{r}^2 + i\omega c\ell^2 + k\ell^2} \tag{62}$$

Equation (62) can be written in the standard form for vibration of systems with one dynamic degree of freedom by writing its numerator as

$$F_1 = F_1^R + iF_1^I = \mathrm{mod}\,F_1 e^{-i\beta}$$

and the denominator as

$$\frac{(1/K)e^{-i\alpha}}{\sqrt{\left[1-(w/w_n)^2\right]^2 + (2\zeta w/w_n)^2}}$$

so that

$$x_1 = \mathrm{Re}\, X_1 e^{i\omega t}$$

is, from equation (62),

$$x_1(t) = \frac{(\mathrm{mod}\, F_1/K)\cos(wt - \alpha - \beta)}{\sqrt{\left[1 - (w/w_n)^2\right]^2 + (2\zeta\, w/w_n)^2}} \tag{63}$$

where, in the above

$$\mathrm{mod}\, F_1 = \sqrt{\left(F_1^R\right)^2 + \left(F_1^I\right)^2}$$

$$\beta = \tan^{-1}\left[-F_1^I / F_1^R\right]$$

$$K = k\ell^2$$

$$\omega_n = \sqrt{K/m\bar{r}^2}$$

$$\zeta = \frac{c\,\ell^2}{2\, m\bar{r}^2\omega_n}$$

$$\alpha = \tan^{-1}\left[\frac{2\zeta\,\omega/\omega_n}{1 - (\omega/\omega_n)^2}\right] \tag{64}$$

In the general case, an analytic closed form inversion of the system equations like that performed above for the simple one dynamic degree-of-freedom system is not possible. Two alternatives exist. The most obvious is just a direct numerical inversion of equation (60). Powerful numerical algorithms are readily available for inverting systems of linear simultaneous algebraic equations.

The alternative solution procedure is *eigenvector*, or *modal, expansion*. Modal expansion is the series solution of the equations of motion, equation (57), in terms of the natural frequencies and mode shapes of the discrete model.

2.3.3.1 NATURAL FREQUENCIES AND MODE SHAPES. By definition, natural frequencies are frequencies of vibration of the free, or unforced, and undamped system. From equation (57), the equations of motion for the free, undamped discrete model are

$$\{-\omega^2[m] + [k]\}|X| = |0|$$

(Here the system model is considered to have a total of L *unknown* degrees of freedom, with N dynamic degrees of freedom (DOF) and $L - N$ static DOF [no mass assigned].)

Denote

$$[D^*(\omega)] = [D]\big|_{[c]=0} = -\omega^2[m] + [k]$$

Then

$$[D^*]|X| = |0| \tag{65}$$

This equation implies that $|X| = 0$ unless $[D^*]$ is singular. But by definition of natural vibration, $|X|$ is not zero. Therefore, the frequencies ω which make $[D^*(\omega)]$ singular are the system natural frequencies; $[D^*]$ is singular if its determinant is zero. Define

$$P(\omega) \equiv \det [D^*(\omega)] \tag{66}$$

$P(\omega)$ is called the *characteristic* polynomial. For N system dynamic degrees of freedom, $P(\omega)$ is a polynomial of order N in ω^2; it has N positive roots in ω. The N positive values of ω which make $P(\omega) = 0$ are the natural frequencies, ω_n

$$P(\omega_n) = 0 \quad n = 1, \ldots N \tag{67}$$

While the number of natural frequencies possessed by continuous systems is always infinite, *the number of natural frequencies of the discrete model is equal to its number* of *dynamic degrees of freedom*. In this regard, it is worth repeating that all real physical systems are at least piece-wise continuous. Therefore, discrete *systems* can be viewed only as discrete *models* of continuous systems; this distinction is not unimportant.

Proceeding, with the N model natural frequencies in hand, a return to equation (65) gives

$$[D^*(\omega_n)]|X| = |0| \tag{68}$$

Now, $|X|$ is not of necessity zero at $\omega = \omega_n$ since $[D^*(\omega)]$ is singular at these frequencies, but it is undefined. Just as with the continuous analysis, the singularity of the coefficient matrix of equation (68) implies a linear dependency within the L equations on the unknown DOF. That is, only $L - 1$ linearly independent equations exist at $\omega = \omega_n$, $n = 1, \ldots, N$, for determining the L unknown components of $|X|$. All that is available from equation (68) are the relative amplitudes, called *mode shapes*, or *eigenvectors*, at each of the N natural frequencies.

The $L \times 1$ mode shape vector is denoted $|\psi_n|$, $n = 1, \ldots N$. It is determined by assuming any one of its L components as known. Then the $L - 1$ equations on the remaining $L - 1$ mode shape components at each n are solved in terms of the one presumed known. That is, assuming arbitrarily that the Lth mode shape component is known, equation (68) is written

$$\begin{bmatrix} D_{11}^* & D_{12}^* & \cdot & \cdot & D_{1\,L-1}^* \\ D_{21}^* & D_{22}^* & & & \cdot \\ \cdot & & & & \\ \cdot & & & & \\ D_{L-11}^* & D_{L-12}^* & \cdot & \cdot & D_{L-1\,L-1}^* \end{bmatrix} \begin{vmatrix} \psi_{1n} \\ \psi_{2n} \\ \cdot \\ \cdot \\ \psi_{L-1n} \end{vmatrix}$$

$$= -\psi_{Ln} \begin{vmatrix} D_{1L}^* \\ D_{2L}^* \\ \cdot \\ \cdot \\ D_{L-1\,L}^* \end{vmatrix} \tag{69}$$

The $(L-1) \times (L-1)$ system of linear algebraic equations, equation (69), is then solved by standard numerical methods for the $(L-1)$ component $|\psi_n|$ for some or all of the N modes of interest.

For the Fig. 6 deckhouse example, the above is simple since L and N are 1. The $[D*]$ matrix from equation (61) is

$$[D*] = -\omega^2 m \bar{r}^2 + k \ell^2$$

which is also the characteristic polynomial $P(\omega)$. $P(\omega_n) = 0$ gives the natural frequency

$$\omega_n = \sqrt{k \ell^2 / m \bar{r}^2}$$

with $n = 1$. The mode shape $|\psi_n|$ is ψ_{11}, which has an arbitrary scale value.

2.3.3.2 MODAL EXPANSION. At this point in the development of the solution for the uniform beam of the last section, a brief description of the modal expansion solution procedure, for that simple case, was followed by its statement. Here, it is considered worthwhile to develop the solution to illustrate a special difficulty that occurs in the more general case.

As before, the complex displacement amplitude vector is first written as a series of the mode shapes weighted by unknown coefficients, A_n.

$$|X| = \sum_{n=1}^{L} A_n |\psi_n| \qquad (70)$$

Substitute equation (70) back into the governing equations (57)

$$\sum_{n=1}^{N} \{ -\omega^2 [m] |\psi_n| + i\omega [c] |\psi_n|$$

$$+ [k] |\psi_n| \} A_n = |F| \qquad (71)$$

Now multiply equation (71) by some $|\psi_m|^T$, with T denoting *transpose* and with m not necessarily equal to n

$$\sum_{n=1}^{N} \{ -\omega^2 |\psi_m|^T [m] |\psi_n| + i\omega |\psi_m|^T [c] |\psi_n|$$

$$+ |\psi_m|^T [k] |\psi_n| \} A_n = |\psi_m|^T |F| \qquad (72)$$

But due to *orthogonality*

$$|\psi_m|^T [m] |\psi_n| = 0 \quad \textit{for } m \neq n$$

Define, for $m = n$,

$$|\psi_m|^T [m] |\psi_m| = M_m \qquad (73)$$

as the mth mode *modal* mass. By equation (73), the summation of the matrix products involving $[m]$ in equation (72) is reduced to a single constant, M_m. Similar reduction of the products involving $[k]$ in equation (72) is accomplished as follows.

By equation (68)

$$\left[D*(\omega_n) \right] |\psi_n| \equiv \{ -\omega_n^2 [m] + [k] \} |\psi_n| = |0|$$

Multiply by $|\psi_m|^T$

$$-\omega_n^2 |\psi_m|^T [m] |\psi_n| + |\psi_m|^T [k] |\psi_n| = |0|$$

Therefore, in view of equation (73)

$$|\psi_m|^T [k] |\psi_n| = \begin{cases} 0 & n \neq m \\ \omega_m^2 M_m & n = m \end{cases}$$

Define

$$K_m = \omega_m^2 M_m \qquad (74)$$

as the mth mode *modal stiffness*, such that

$$\omega_m = \sqrt{K_m / M_m}$$

Also, define

$$|\psi_m|^T |F| = F_m \qquad (75)$$

as the mth mode *modal exciting force*.

Substitute equations (73), (74), and (75) back into equation (72)

$$\left(-\omega^2 M_m + K_m \right) A_m$$

$$+ i\omega \sum_{n=1}^{N} |\psi_m|^T [c] |\psi_n| A_n = F_m \qquad (76)$$

Now, if orthogonality can be employed to reduce the damping term in equation (76) similarly as with the mass and stiffness, then the A_m required in the solution (70) are determined. However, orthogonality on the damping matrix does not, in general, exist for $N > 1$. It exists only in special cases. For example, if $[c]$ is proportional to $[m]$ and/or $[k]$, then orthogonality exists (c was proportional to both k and m in the simple distributed model of Section 2.1; that provided the mode shape orthogonality required at equation [36]). That is, for

$$[c] = \gamma_n [k] + \delta_n [m] \qquad (77)$$

where γ_n and δ_n are constants which are allowed to vary only from mode to mode, then, in equation (76)

$$|\psi_m|^T [c] |\psi_m| = \gamma_m K_m + \delta_m M_m \equiv C_m \qquad (78)$$

C_m is called the *modal damping coefficient*. Presuming C_m to exist, the A_m are then, from equation (76),

$$A_m = \frac{F_m}{-\omega^2 M_m + iw\, C_m + K_m}$$

or

$$A_m = \frac{F_m / K_m}{1 - (\omega/\omega_m)^2 + 2i\zeta_m \omega/\omega_m} \qquad (79)$$

where

$$\zeta_m = \frac{C_m}{2M_m\omega_m} = \frac{\gamma_m\omega_m}{2} + \frac{\delta_m}{2\omega_m} \qquad (80)$$

ζ_m is the mth mode *modal damping factor*. Substituting equation (79) into equation (70) completes the derivation

$$|X| = \sum_{n=1}^{L} |X_n^{\bullet}| e^{-i(\alpha_n+\beta_n)}$$

with

$$|X| = \frac{\mathrm{mod}\, F_n / K_n}{\sqrt{\left[1-(\omega/\omega_n)^2\right]^2 + (2\zeta_n\omega/\omega_n)^2}} |\psi_n| \qquad (81)$$

$|x(t)|$ follows as

$$|x(t)| = \mathrm{Re}|X| e^{i\omega t}$$
$$= \sum_{n=1}^{L} |X_n| \cos(\omega t - \alpha_n - \beta_n) \qquad (82)$$

Here, α_n and β_n are the modal phase angles

$$\beta_n = \tan^{-1}\left[-F_n^I / F_n^R\right]$$

$$\alpha_n = \tan^{-1}\left[\frac{2\zeta_n(\omega/\omega_n)}{1-(\omega/\omega_n)^2}\right]$$

Equations (81) and (82) are general equations that have wide application to ship vibration problems, as discussed in Section 3. These equations again confirm that modal expansion can be viewed as just a superposition of the responses of N equivalent one-DOF systems representing each of the N modes of the discrete model. The only difference between the above solution for continuous and that for discrete models is the length of the series. The continuous case, having infinite degrees of freedom, generates an infinite series.

The restriction imposed upon damping at equation (77) for $N > 1$ must also be observed in continuous analysis; this difficulty did not appear explicitly in the last section because the beam with uniform properties, in fact, possesses proportional damping automatically.

The restriction on damping is severe. For the internal material damping of structural systems, a damping matrix proportional to stiffness can be justified; the simple theory used in the last section for allowing for material damping of the continuous beam leads to this conclusion. However, where other sources of damping are also present, proportionality is usually destroyed, and, in such cases, the modal expansion, equation (81), does not exist, theoretically.

Nevertheless, temptations exist for applying the modal formula to models where proportional damping cannot, in reality, be justified. Ship vibration is a typical example. Three potential advantages of modal expansion over the direct numerical inversion approach, equation (60), exist, particularly for large models:

1. The solution, equation (81), is in terms of arbitrary exciting frequency, ω. A summation must merely be performed to evaluate the model response at any frequency of interest; the direct inversion requires complete numerical reanalysis of each variation of ω.

2. In general, a discrete model of a continuous system is accurate for only the system modes within a limited frequency range. That is, while typically the lowest modes of an N degree of freedom model should represent the same modes of the continuous system with accuracy, the Nth mode of the discrete model would be expected to bear little resemblance to the Nth mode of the continuous system. A direct inversion theoretically includes the responses of all N model modes. While including the erroneous model modes may not actually contaminate the results of the analysis, it is certainly inefficient to carry them. In modal analysis, the series can be truncated at levels where modeling inaccuracy becomes pronounced without sacrificing the accuracy of the analysis within the frequency range for which the model was constructed. This means that only a relative few of the N natural frequencies and mode shapes of the discrete model need be evaluated in order to predict the system vibration characteristics of concern.

3. The semianalytical form of the modal expansion provides insight into the relative contributions of the elements of mass, stiffness, damping, and excitation influencing a particular vibration problem. This visibility is not available with a purely numerical inversion of the model equations.

Returning again to the deckhouse model in Figs. 6 and 7, the modal expansion of the one dynamic degree-of-freedom model is just the analytic solution, equation (63), as comparison with equations (81) and (82) confirms. The deckhouse response predicted by the simple one-degree-of-freedom model is interesting, however. For simplicity, assume that the hull girder vibration in the vicinity of the house, Fig. 6, is rather "flat." That is, assume that the aftermost hull girder nodal point at frequency ω is far enough forward of the house that $w(\xi_1, t) \approx w(\xi_2, t)$ in Fig. 6; the house base experiences a pure vertical translation. Then, in equation (62), with $X_2 = X_3 \equiv X$,

$$F_1 = -\omega^2 m\bar{\xi}X$$

Taking X real (which implies a reference phase of zero)

$$\mathrm{mod}\,F_1 = \omega^2 m\bar{\xi}X \quad and \quad \beta = \pi$$

Also, assume that the house is in resonance at ω. The house rocking vibration, by equation (63), is then

$$x_1(t) = \frac{\omega_n^2 m\bar{\xi}X/K}{2\zeta} \cos(\omega t - 3\pi/2) \qquad (83)$$

with $\alpha = \pi/2$ at resonance. By equation (50) the fore-and-aft vibration displacement at the house top is

$$u(h, t) = x_1(t)h$$

Substitute equation (83)

$$\frac{u(h,t)}{X} = \frac{\omega_n^2 m \overline{\xi} h}{2K\zeta} \cos(\omega t + \pi/2)$$

But $\omega_n^2 = K/m\overline{r}^2$, which gives

$$\frac{u(h,t)}{X} = \frac{\overline{\xi} h}{2\zeta\overline{r}^2} \cos(\omega t + \pi/2) \tag{84}$$

Taking as typical values of the data in (84), $\overline{\xi}/\overline{r} = 0.75$, $h/\overline{r} = 1.333$, and $\zeta = 0.05$, the house top fore-and-aft displacement is:

$$\frac{u(h,t)}{X} = 10\cos(\omega t + \pi/2) \tag{85}$$

This simple analysis implies that the fore-and-aft vibration at the house top can be 10 times the vertical vibration on main deck at resonant conditions. This is not at all out of line with observations. Unacceptable fore-and-aft vibration levels in deckhouses, accompanied by relatively low level vibration of the hull girder, and elsewhere in a ship have been a common occurrence.

2.3 Propeller Exciting Forces. The propeller excitation in the foregoing has been characterized as a simple force concentrated at some point near the aft end of the hull girder. This is acceptable only for elementary demonstration purposes. Propeller excitation is a complicated combination of concentrated forces and moments acting at the propeller hub, plus a distribution of fluctuating pressure acting over the after-hull surfaces. The concentrated propeller bearing forces and moments are largely responsible for the vibration of main propulsion machinery and shafting systems but are not unimportant, in general, as a source of hull vibratory excitation. The usually dominant hull excitation of modern ships is, however, the propeller-induced hull surface pressure field. This is particularly true when any degree of fluctuating sheet cavitation occurs on the propeller blades, which is more often the rule than the exception. The fundamental concepts and theory of propeller bearing forces and propeller-induced hull surface forces are treated in the following.

2.3.1 Propeller Bearing Forces. Consider Fig. 8, which depicts a propeller blade rotating with angular velocity Ω in the clockwise direction, looking forward. By virtue of the rotation through the circumferentially nonuniform wake, the spanwise blade lift distribution, $L(r, \theta)$, fluctuates with time, or with blade position angle $\theta = -\Omega t$. It is of interest to determine the three force and three moment components in the propeller hub produced by the time varying lift distributions of all N blades acting simultaneously. Toward this purpose, define the complex function

$$g(r, \theta; p) = -L(r, \theta)e^{ip\theta}e^{j\beta_G} \tag{86}$$

Here, i and j both denote $\sqrt{-1}$, but they are to be treated as independent in all algebraic manipulations; the reason for this artifice is only for compactness of nota-

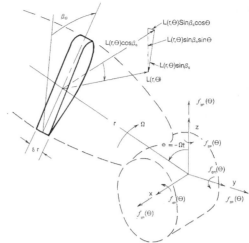

Fig. 8 Propeller blade-element forces.

tion. β_G in equation (86) is the geometric pitch angle of the blade section at r, and p is an integer to be assigned later.

The function $g(r, \theta; p)$ by equation (86) represents a *pseudo-lift* distribution on one blade of the N-bladed propeller. The effect of all N blades acting simultaneously is achieved by replacing θ by $\theta + 2\pi(k-1)/N$ in equation (86) and summing over k. This operation defines a new complex lift function representing the collective effects of the N blades.

$$G(r, \theta; p) \equiv \sum_{k=1}^{N} g(r, \theta + 2\pi(k-1)/N; p)$$

$$= -\sum_{k=1}^{N} L(r, \theta +$$

$$+ 2\pi(k-1)/N)e^{ip\theta}e^{\frac{2\pi i(k_m-1)}{N}}e^{j\beta_G} \tag{87}$$

Now, the circumferential wake nonuniformity appears from the blade to be very nearly periodic in time, with fundamental period $T = 2\pi/\Omega$. With the assumption of linearity, the lift distribution, $L(r, \theta) \equiv L(r, t)$, is also periodic with the same period. $L(r, \theta)$ can therefore be written in the Fourier series

$$L(r, \theta) = L_0(r) + \text{Re} \sum_{q=1}^{\infty} L_q(r)e^{iq\theta} \tag{88}$$

Here, $L_q(r)$ is the qth harmonic complex lift amplitude of the blade section at radius r; $L_0(r)$ is the steady lift distribution associated with steady thrust and torque. A choice in procedures for determining the $L_q(r)$ harmonics is available on specification of the corresponding harmonics of the wake inflow (see Section 3). It is presumed at this point that a sufficient number of the $L_q(r)$ harmonics are available from some source.

An alternative representation of equation (88), which is useful for insertion into equation (87), is

$$L(r,\theta) = L_0(r) + \frac{1}{2}\sum_{q=1}^{\infty}\left[L_q(r)e^{iq\theta} + \overline{L}_q(r)e^{-iq\theta}\right] \quad (89)$$

where the overbar denotes complex conjugate. Discarding the steady lift and substituting equation (89) into equation (87) produces

$$G(r,\theta;p) =$$
$$-\frac{1}{2}e^{j\beta_G}\sum_{q=1}^{\infty}\left[L_q(r)e^{i(q+p)\theta}\sum_{k=1}^{N}e^{\frac{i(q+p)2\pi(k-1)}{N}}\right.$$
$$\left. + \overline{L}_q(r)e^{-i(q-p)\theta}\sum_{k=1}^{N}e^{\frac{-i(q-p)2\pi(k-1)}{N}}\right] \quad (90)$$

But it can be easily verified that the k summations appearing in equation (90) are equal to zero if $q \pm p$ is not some integer multiple of N, say mN, and the summations are equal to N for $q \pm p = mN$. Using these facts, equation (90) reduces to a sum over m alone

$$G(r,\theta;p) = -\frac{N}{2}e^{j\beta_G}\sum_{m=1}^{\infty}\left[L_{mN-p}(r)e^{imN\theta}\right.$$
$$\left. + \overline{L}_{mN+p}(r)e^{-imN\theta}\right] \quad (91)$$

The bearing forces $f_{ip}(\theta), i = 1, \ldots, 6$, Fig. 8, are now given in terms of $G(r, \theta; p)$ from equation (91) as

$$f_{1p}(\theta) = \mathrm{Re}_j\int_{r=rh}^{R}G(r,\theta;0)dr$$

$$f_{2p}(\theta) = \mathrm{Re}_i\,\mathrm{Im}_j\int_{r=rh}^{R}G(r,\theta;1)dr$$

$$f_{3p}(\theta) = \mathrm{Im}_i\,\mathrm{Im}_j\int_{r=rh}^{R}G(r,\theta;1)dr$$

$$f_{4p}(\theta) = \mathrm{Im}_j\int_{r=rh}^{R}rG(r,\theta;0)dr$$

$$f_{5p}(\theta) = \mathrm{Re}_i\,\mathrm{Re}_j\int_{r=rh}^{R}rG(r,\theta;1)dr$$

$$f_{6p}(\theta) = \mathrm{Im}_i\,\mathrm{Re}_j\int_{r=rh}^{R}rG(r,\theta,1)dr \quad (92)$$

The prefixes Re and Im refer to the real and imaginary parts of the complex quantities involving i and j; the complex lift harmonic is $Lq = Lq^R + iLq^I$ in this regard.

As an example, consider the vertical bearing force, f_{3p}. Equations (91) and (92) give

$$f_{3p}(\theta) = \mathrm{Im}\left\{-\frac{N}{2}\sum_{m=1}^{\infty}\int_{r=rh}^{R}\sin\beta_G\left[L_{mN-1}(r)e^{imN\theta}\right.\right.$$
$$\left.\left. + \overline{L}_{mN+1}(r)e^{-imN\theta}\right]dr\right\}$$

Using the facts that

$$\mathrm{Im}\,Z = -\mathrm{Re}\,iZ$$

and

$$\mathrm{Im}\,\overline{Z} = \mathrm{Re}\,iZ$$

$$f_{3p}(\theta) = -\mathrm{Re}\left\{\frac{N}{2i}\sum_{m=1}^{\infty}e^{imN\theta}\int_{R=rh}^{R}\left[L_{mN-1}(r)\right.\right.$$
$$\left.\left. - L_{mN+1}(r)\right]\sin\beta_G\,dr\right\}$$

This formula differs from that given by Tsakonas, Breslin, and Miller (1967), for example, only in sign. The sign difference is due to the fact that positive lift is here taken as that with forward axial component, in the usual sense. This is opposite to the convention of the Tsakonas et al.

The following important facts should be observed from equations (91) and (92).

1. Propeller bearing forces are periodic with fundamental frequency equal to the propeller angular velocity times the number of blades. The fundamental frequency, $N\Omega$, is called *blade-rate* frequency. The bearing forces, as written in equations (91) and (92), are composed of terms at blade-rate frequency, plus all of its integer multiples, or harmonics, $mN\Omega$.

2. Only certain terms, or harmonics, of the unsteady blade lift, and therefore of the hull wake, contribute to the bearing forces. While the forces on a single blade consist of components corresponding to all wake harmonics, a filtering occurs when the blade forces superimpose at the propeller hub. Equations (91) and (92) show that the unsteady thrust and torque, f_{1p} and f_{4p}, depend only on the lift, or wake, harmonics that are integer multiples of blade number. The lateral forces and moments, on the other hand, are produced entirely by the wake harmonics corresponding to integer multiples of blade number, plus and minus one.

2.3.2 Propeller-Induced Hull Surface Pressures and Forces.

A thorough understanding of the hull surface pressure distributions produced by a propeller, and of the integration to resultant hull surface forces, is attained only with a considerable expenditure of effort. The subject is very complex. Nevertheless, much has been accomplished since the pioneering experimental work of Lewis (1973) in both understanding hull surface excitation and developing methods for predicting it.

2.3.2.1 UNIFORM INFLOW CONDITIONS. It is useful to begin with the simplest possible case: the pressure induced on a flat plate by a propeller operating in a uniform inflow. This is depicted in Fig. 9, which is a sketch of the water tunnel arrangement from which the data shown in Fig. 10 were measured (Denny, 1967).

Two different three-bladed propellers were used in the experiments. The propellers were identical in all respects, including performance, except one had blades double the thickness of the other. With the assumption of linearity, this allowed the independent effects of blade

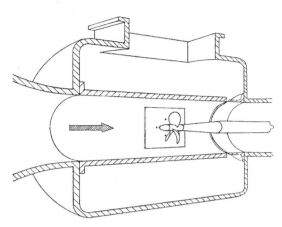

Fig. 9 Flat-plate pressure measurements.

thickness and blade lift to be distinguished from the experimental data recorded with the two propellers. The leftside plots in Fig. 10 show the amplitude and phase of the plate pressure induced by blade thickness; the rightside plots correspond to blade lift. The predictions of theories made available in the late 1960s are also shown in Fig. 10.

The pressure data shown in Fig. 10 correspond to blade-rate frequency. Just as in the case of bearing forces, all multiples of blade-rate frequency also occur, but the higher harmonics become negligible quickly for the uniform wake case. The phase indicated in Fig. 10 is defined as the position angle of the propeller blade

nearest the plate (see Fig. 9) when the pressure is positive (compressive) maximum; positive angle is defined as counterclockwise, looking forward. With this definition, the phase relative to a single cycle of the three-cycle-per-revolution blade-rate signal is obtained by multiplying the phase angles in Fig. 10 by 3. This quickly confirms that the blade thickness pressure is approximately in-phase up- and downstream of the propeller; it is an even function in x, approximately. On the other hand, a large phase shift occurs in the pressure due to blade lift up- and downstream; it behaves as an odd function in x, approximately. This behavior suggests some substantial cancellation in the lift associated pressure, at least, on integration to the net resultant vertical force on the plate. Actually, if the plate is infinite in extent, the thickness pressure and the lift pressure both independently integrate to produce identically zero net vertical force on the plate. This fact is a demonstration of the Breslin condition (Breslin, 1959). This was established by integrating theoretical pressures induced by a noncavitating propeller operating in uniform inflow over the infinite flat plate and showing the identically zero result.

Figure 11 is a contour plot of the blade-rate pressure amplitude from a similar but different uniform wake, flat plate experiment (Breslin & Kowalski, 1964). Here, only amplitude is shown; the phase shift distribution responsible for the cancellation on integration is not apparent from Fig. 11. Figures 10 and 11 clearly imply that propeller-induced hull surface pressure is highly localized in the immediate vicinity of the propeller; the pressure is reduced to a small percentage of its maximum value within one propeller radius of the maximum. There is a tendency, on the basis of this observation, to draw the false conclusion that resultant forces occurring in the general ship case should be similarly concentrated on the hull in the near region of the propeller. This common misconception is explained by the considerations of the following section.

2.3.2.2 CIRCUMFERENTIALLY NONUNIFORM WAKE EFFECTS. It was shown in the propeller bearing force theory that

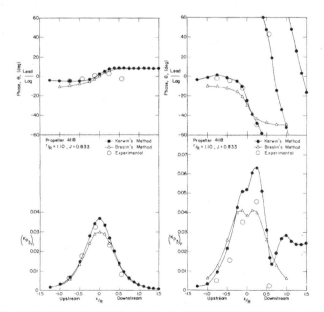

(a) — Comparisons of Theoretical and Experimental Values, Thickness Contribution, r/R = 1.10, J = 0.833   (b) — Comparisons of Theoretical and Experimental Values, Loading Contribution, r/R = 1.10, J = 0.833

Fig. 10 Flat-plate pressure amplitude and phase distributions. **(A)** Comparisons of theoretical and experimental values, thickness contribution, r/R = 1.10, J = 0.833. **(B)** Comparisons of theoretical and experimental values, loading contribution, r/R = 1.10, J = 0.833.

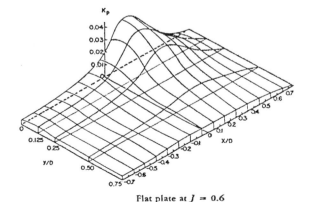

Flat plate at J = 0.6

Fig. 11 Flat-plate pressure contours. Flat plate at J = 0.6.

only certain shaft-rate harmonics of the nonuniform wake contribute to the blade-rate bearing force harmonics. In the case of the propeller-induced hull surface excitation, the entire infinity of shaft-rate wake harmonics contribute to each blade-rate excitation harmonic. But particular wake harmonics are nevertheless dominant, with the degree of dominance depending primarily on hull form. This will be considered in more detail later.

The pressure distribution corresponding to the wake operating propeller (without cavitation) has a very similar appearance to the uniform wake case. Figure 12, from Vorus (1974), shows calculated and measured blade-rate pressure amplitude at points on a section in the propeller plane of a model of the DE-1040. It was assumed in both of the pressure calculations shown that the hull surface appeared to the propeller as a flat plate of infinite extent.

The upper part of Fig. 12 shows the measured pressure produced by the wake-operating propeller, along with the corresponding calculated results. Both blade-rate pressure calculations include the uniform wake effects of steady blade lift and blade thickness (see Figs. 10 and 11), plus the contributions from the circumfer-

entially nonuniform part of the wake. The nonuniform wake contribution is represented by wake harmonics 1 through 8 (the "zeroth" wake harmonic component referred to in Fig. 12 is equivalent to the steady blade-lift and blade-thickness components).

The lower part of Fig. 12 shows a breakdown of the calculated blade-rate pressure distribution from above, as indicated, into contributions from the uniform wake components (steady blade lift and blade thickness) and nonuniform wake components (sum of unsteady lift harmonics 1 to 8). The important point is that the pressure is dominated by the uniform wake effects; the pressure associated with the uniform wake from the lower part of Fig. 12 is essentially identical to the total pressure shown in the upper. The nonuniform wake contribution to the blade-rate pressure is buried at a low level within the large uniform wake component.

Interestingly, the integral of the pressure to a vertical force on the relatively flat stern has an entirely different character with regard to the relative contributions of the uniform and nonuniform wake components. This is shown in Fig. 13, also from Vorus (1974). Here, other than the first column result in Fig. 13, the hull surface is modeled accurately with zero pressure satisfied on the water surface. The second column in Fig. 13 shows the total blade-rate vertical hull surface force calculated on the DE-1040. The succeeding 10 columns show the contributions to the force from blade thickness and the first nine harmonics of blade lift. Figure 13 shows that it is the nonuniform wake components, which are small

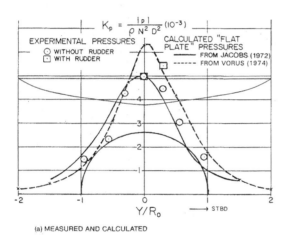

(a) MEASURED AND CALCULATED

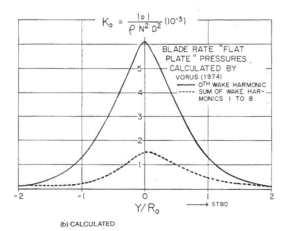

(b) CALCULATED

Fig. 12 Blade-rate flat-plate pressures on destroyer stern, station 19.

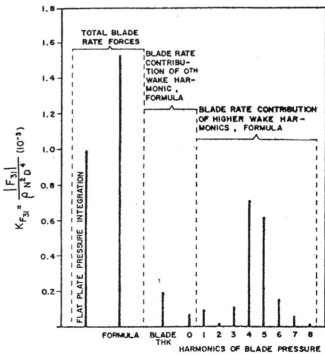

Fig. 13 Calculated blade-rate vertical hull surface forces on destroyer stern (DE 1040).

in the surface pressure, that dominate the integrated surface force. The large uniform wake pressure due to steady blade lift and blade thickness integrates almost to zero over the (almost) flat stern surface (the Breslin condition), leaving a blade-rate exciting force due almost entirely to the wake harmonics of orders in the vicinity of blade number (the DE-1040 propeller has five blades).

Actually, the Breslin condition, as established by Breslin (1959) for the uniform inflow case, can be generalized to cover the nonuniform inflow case as well. It can be stated that, for the case of the general noncavitating propeller, the unsteady vertical force induced on an infinite plate above the propeller is equal and opposite to the unsteady vertical force acting on the propeller; the net vertical force on the plate/propeller combination is identically zero. This, of course, covers the uniform inflow case since the vertical forces on the plate and propeller are both individually zero. The DE-1040 example of Fig. 13 is a good approximate demonstration of the nonuniform inflow case. It was shown by equations (91) and (92) that the vertical bearing force is produced exclusively by the blade-order multiple harmonics of the wake, plus and minus one. For the propeller operating in a wake under an infinite flat plate, the vertical force on the plate, being equal but opposite to the vertical bearing force, must also have to be composed exclusively of the blade-order wake harmonics, plus and minus one. These harmonics are obvious in the DE-1040 vertical surface force spectrum of Fig. 13; the DE-1040 stern would be characterized as flat plate–like. With five blades, the fourth and sixth harmonics dominate the vertical blade-rate surface force, along with the fifth. Amplification of the fifth harmonic is due to the presence of the water surface off the waterplane ending aft.

With regard to the degree of cancellation in the net vertical force on the DE-1040, the bearing force amplitude was calculated to be 0.00205. Its vector addition with the surface force of 0.0015 amplitude produced a net force of amplitude equal to 0.00055, which reflects substantial cancellation. It is noteworthy that Lewis (1963) measured a net vertical force of amplitude 0.0004 on a model of the same vessel at Massachusetts Institute of Technology. In the case of the DE-1040, the surface force is smaller in amplitude than the bearing force, but this is not a generality.

At any rate, the characteristics demonstrated in Figs. 11, 12, and 13 clearly indicate that measured surface pressure is a very poor measure of merit of propeller vibratory excitation. Hull vibration is produced largely by the integral of the surface pressure, the severity of which is not necessarily well represented by the magnitude of the local surface pressure distribution.

This fact also implies the level of difficulty that one should expect in attempting to evaluate hull surface forces by numerically integrating measured hull surface pressure. The measurements would have to be extremely precise so as to accurately capture the details of the small nonuniform wake pressure components embedded in the large, but essentially inconsequential, uniform wake pressure component.

One other relevant aspect with regard to this last point deserves consideration. Returning to Fig. 12, it was noted that the hull was assumed to be an infinite flat plate for purposes of the pressure calculation. This assumption might be expected to result in reasonable satisfaction of the hull surface boundary condition in the very near field of the propeller. So long as the pressure decays rapidly within the propeller near field, reasonably accurate estimates of the pressure maxima might therefore be expected with the flat-plate assumption. Figure 12 confirms this. All of the pressure measurement points, where good agreement with calculation is shown, are relatively close to the propeller and well inside the waterplane boundaries.

Outside the waterplane boundaries, the relief effects of the water free surface impose a very different boundary condition than that of a rigid flat plate. Hull surface pressure in the vicinity of the waterplane extremities would therefore be poorly approximated by the infinite flat-plate assumption (Vorus, 1976). The overall validity of the flat-plate assumption should therefore depend on the relative importance of surface pressure near the waterplane extremities, outside the immediate propeller near field.

From the point of view of the pressure maxima, the very rapid decay of the dominant uniform wake part justifies the flat-plate assumption. On the other hand, accuracy of the integrated hull surface forces depends on accurate prediction of the small nonuniform wake pressure components. While these components are relatively small, they also decay much more slowly with distance away from the propeller. It is obvious from Fig. 12 that the pressure persisting laterally to the water surface (which is assumed to be a continuation of the flat plate in the calculations) is due entirely to the nonuniform wake components. These small pressures persist over large distances and integrate largely in-phase to produce the hull surface forces.

The flat-plate assumption should therefore be less reliable for the prediction of hull surface forces, than for hull surface pressure maxima. This is supported by Fig. 13. The first column on Fig. 13 represents the vertical force amplitude calculated by integrating the calculated "flat-plate" pressures over the DE-1040 afterbody.

The second column in Fig. 13 is the vertical force calculated using a reciprocity principle (Vorus, 1974) that satisfies the hull and water surface boundary conditions much more closely than does the flat-plate approximation. While some slight differences in the wake used in the two calculations were discovered, the main difference in the two total force levels shown is due primarily to misrepresentation of the water surface in the calculation using the flat-plate assumption.

The fact that the most important nonuniform wake part of the surface pressure acts over a large surface area actually suggests that total integrated hull surface forces are not the best measure of hull vibratory excitation either. It is the scalar product of pressure distribution and vibratory mode shape represented in the generalized forces of equations (41) or (82) that would properly allow for "propeller excitability" in the context of the discussion of Fig. 5 (Vorus, 1971).

2.3.2.3 CAVITATION EFFECTS.   The propeller cavitation of concern from the standpoint of vibratory excitation is fluctuating sheet cavitation that expands and collapses on the back of each blade in a repeating fashion, revolution after revolution (Fig. 14). The sheet expansion typically commences as the blade enters the region of high wake in the top part of the propeller disk. Collapse occurs on leaving the high-wake region in a violent and unstable fashion, with the final remnants of the sheet typically trailed out behind in the blade tip vortex. The sheet may envelope almost the entire back of the outboard blade sections at its maximum extent. For large ship propellers, sheet average thicknesses are on the order of 10 cm, with maxima on the order of 25 cm occurring near the blade tip just before collapse.

The type of cavitation shown in Fig. 14, while of catastrophic appearance, is usually not deleterious from the standpoint of ship propulsive performance. The blade continues to lift effectively; the blade suction-side surface pressure is maintained at the cavity pressure where

cavitation occurs. The propeller bearing forces may be largely unaffected relative to noncavitating values for the same reason. The cavitation may or may not be erosive, depending largely on the degree of *cloud cavitation* (a mist of small bubbles) accompanying the sheet dynamics. The devastating appearance of fluctuating sheet cavitation is manifest consistently only in the field pressure that it radiates and the noise and vibration that it thereby produces. The level of hull surface excitation induced by a cavitating propeller can be easily an order of magnitude larger than typical noncavitating levels. The Breslin condition does not apply in the cavitating case, and vertical hull surface forces due to unsteady cavitation typically exceed vertical propeller bearing forces by large amounts.

Fluctuating sheet cavitation can be characterized as an unsteady blade thickness effect from the standpoint of field pressure radiation. Any unsteady blade thickness effects associated with the noncavitating propeller are higher order, as demonstrated in the preceding. Furthermore, the steady average cavity thickness (zeroth harmonic) produces field pressure on the order of that produced by the bare blade. It is the sourcelike volume expansion and collapse associated with the cavity unsteadiness that produces the large blade-rate radiated pressure and its harmonic multiples.

Just as with the unsteadiness of blade lift in the noncavitating case, the cavitating hull forces are produced primarily by the pressure components associated with the higher cavitation harmonics of order near blade number and the blade number multiples. For the same maximum cavity volume, the *shorter* the duration of the cavitation, the higher is its high harmonic content.

Strength in the high harmonics of the cavitation spectrum results in significant excitation at the blade-rate multiples; slow convergence of the blade-rate excitation series is a characteristic of cavitating propellers.

In view of the importance of the various sets of harmonics involved in propeller excitation, one important distinction between the cavitating and noncavitating cases should be recognized at this point. In the noncavitating case, a one-to-one relationship exists between the harmonics of the circumferentially nonuniform wake and the harmonics of blade lift; the assumption of linearity, which makes each blade-lift harmonic a function of only the corresponding wake harmonic, has been established as valid because of the typically small flow perturbation in the noncavitating case. Such a linear relationship does not exist between the wake harmonics and the cavitation volume harmonics. Certainly, it is the nonuniform wake that almost solely produces the fluctuating sheet cavitation. But sheet cavitation growth has been found theoretically to be most responsive only to the first few harmonics of the wake. The sheet cavitation, which is produced mainly by the low harmonic content of the wake, typically completes its cycle within a relatively small fraction of one propeller revolution. The volume associated with this rapid expansion and

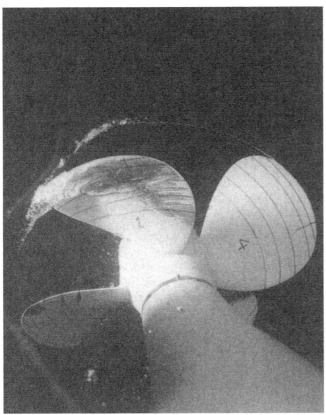

Fig. 14 Fluctuating sheet cavitation.

collapse has much more strength in its high harmonics than does the part of the wake that produces it.

As an aside, it may someday prove to be a fortunate circumstance that cavitation effects, which are most important in the propeller vibratory excitation problem, depend most strongly on only the gross features (low harmonics) of the nonuniform wake. Unlike the fine detail of the wake to which noncavitating forces are most sensitive, some hope may be held for rational prediction of gross wake characteristics with useful accuracy.

The character of the cavitation-induced hull pressure field differs from the noncavitating case in one important respect. The multiple blade-rate pressure components produced by the higher cavity harmonics, which are dominant in the integrated forces, are no longer mere "squiggles" imbedded in a vastly larger zeroth harmonic field. The now-large pressure components from the cavitation unsteadiness should be more accurately captured in measurements of total pressure signals. For this reason, measurements of cavitation-induced point pressure would be expected to be a more meaningful measure of vibratory excitation than noncavitating pressure. However, the filtering action of the hull surface on integration still appears to be capable of producing inconsistencies between point pressure and integrated force levels. Higher-order cavitation harmonics with strength in the pressure distribution will be modified in strength by the surface integration, to different degrees. Different weightings of the various pressure harmonic components could logically result in a superposition of drastically different character in the force resultants. From case to case, measured pressure of levels inconsistent with the levels of the forces that they integrate to produce should not be unexpected.

Greater accuracy should also be achievable in numerically integrating measured cavitation-induced pressure to attain hull surface force estimates. This is, again, because the size of the important pressure components is relatively greater than in the noncavitating case. However, coverage of a large area of the model surface with pressure transducers should be required in view of the very slow attenuation of the cavitation induced pressure signal. In this regard, whether forces or pressures are the interest, it is no doubt most important that boundary conditions be modeled accurately, either in analysis or experiments. Theory indicates, for example, that due to the slow spatial pressure attenuation associated with the cavitation volume source strength, surface pressure, even in the immediate propeller vicinity, can be overestimated by a factor on the order of four in typical cases if the rigid wall boundary condition is employed at the water surface.

A basis for estimating excitation forces from cavitating propellers is the general reciprocity theorem applied by Vorus (1971, 1974). The theorem expresses reciprocal relations between forces and motions in linear dynamical systems. For the case of hull surface excitation forces resulting from propeller cavitation,

$$\left(\frac{F_m}{\dot{q}(z)}\right) = \left(\frac{p(z)}{V_m}\right) \tag{93}$$

where z denotes a position in the propeller plane, and F_m denotes the amplitude of a harmonically oscillating modal excitation force on the hull resulting from a similarly oscillating cavitation source having volume-rate amplitude, $\dot{q}$. On the right side, the pressure, p, is that induced at the propeller by the hull modal velocity, V_m. The idea is that the unknown force per unit cavitation volume velocity on the hull is equal to the pressure in the propeller plane per unit forced hull motion, which can be either measured or calculated.

Reciprocity relationships similar to equation (93) also exist for the noncavitating hull surface forces.

Approximate formulas for evaluating propeller-induced vibratory forces are proposed in Section 3.

2.4 Underwater Radiated Noise. The sources of ship vibration, as well as ship vibration itself, are "noisy." This is especially true with regard to noise radiated subsurface through the liquid medium. Underwater radiated noise is particularly important in vessels involved in military operations, where easy detection from far distances can be fatal.

2.4.1 Cavitation Dynamics as a Noise Source. The principal source of ship underwater noise is propeller cavitation. This occurs indirectly as structure-born noise from vessel vibration produced by propeller cavitation. But the most important source of underwater radiated noise is that due directly to the dynamics of fluctuating sheet cavity volumes on the rotating propeller blades (see Fig. 14). The large cavitation-induced field pressure cited in the last section as most important in producing vibratory surface forces on the near-field hull boundaries also produces large noise levels in both the near- and far-fields of the vessel. The first line of defense against excessive noise in military vessels is effective suppression of propeller cavitation dynamics, and this is effectively achieved in modern U.S. warships.

First considerations in *analysis* of propeller cavitation as a vibration and noise source are developed in the next section. The effort in this current section is to lay some of the theoretical groundwork for understanding the basics of the problem. The principal acoustic references used here are the fundamental texts of Beranek (1960) and Kinsler and Frey (1962).

Propeller sheet cavitation manifests in the field as the pressure from the expanding and collapsing, and rotating, cavity volume distributions on the propeller blades. This cavity dynamic is assumed to be periodic, with the same pattern repeating on each propeller blade revolution after revolution. It is composed theoretically of distributions of multipole singularities (i.e., monopoles, dipoles, quadripoles, etc.) with the content in the successively higher-order singularities reflecting the increasing complexity of the cavitation pattern at the local level. But the sound pressure in the field produced by the higher-order multipole content diminishes most quickly with distance away from the propeller. The field pressure is dominated more and more by the fundamental monopole, or source, component of the distribution as distance increases. In the far field, which is most critical from the standpoint of acoustic detectability, propeller sheet cavitation can therefore be conceptually characterized as set of N symmetrically spaced monopoles, or point sources, attached to and rotating with each of the N blades. The strength of each rotating source is $q(\theta)$, with $\theta = -\Omega t$; refer to Section 2.3 and Fig. 14. The strength of each point source is the periodically pulsating velocity of the cavity volume variation $\dot{\forall}(\theta)$. As a Fourier series

$$q(\theta) = \text{Re} \sum_{p=1}^{\infty} \dot{\forall}_p e^{ip\theta} \qquad (94)$$

Following the development of the propeller bearing force formula in Section 2.3, equation (94) is first written in the alternative form

$$q(\theta) = \frac{1}{2} \sum_{p=1}^{\infty} \left[\dot{\forall}_p e^{ip\theta} + \overline{\dot{\forall}}_p e^{-ip\theta} \right] \qquad (95)$$

Now replace θ by $\theta + 2\pi(k-1)/N$ in equation (95) and sum over N to obtain the source strength, $Q(\theta)$, representing all blades collectively.

$$Q(\theta) = \frac{1}{2} \sum_{p=1}^{\infty} \left[\dot{\forall}_p e^{ip\theta} \sum_{k=1}^{N} e^{\frac{2\pi ip(k-1)}{N}} + \right.$$
$$\left. + \overline{\dot{\forall}}_p e^{-ip\theta} \sum_{k=1}^{N} e^{\frac{-2\pi ip(k-1)}{N}} \right] \qquad (96)$$

But as developed on Section 2.3, the k summations in equation (96) are zero if $\pm p$ is not an integer multiple of N, say mN, and the k summations are equal to N for $\pm p = mN$. This reduces equation (96) to:

$$Q(\theta) = N\text{Re} \sum_{n=1}^{\infty} \dot{\forall}_{nN} e^{inN\theta} \qquad (97)$$

$\theta = -\Omega t$ in equation (97), consistent with Section 2.3.

With $\dot{\forall}_q$ denoting the complete set of single-blade cavity volume velocity harmonics, as complex amplitudes, N the propeller blade number, and Ω the propeller angular velocity, $N\Omega$ is the blade-rate frequency fundamental. Summing over the multiple blades has therefore resulted in filtering of the complete cavitation volume velocity spectrum to just the blade-rate frequency component and its harmonics, as seen in the propeller far-field.

2.4.2 Far-Field Sound Pressure. The dynamics of this net cavitating propeller source produces an oscillating pressure, $p(r, t)$ in the field, where r is the radius from the source center. This *sound pressure* is governed by the general *acoustic wave equation*

$$\frac{\partial^2 p}{\partial t^2} = c^2 \nabla^2 p \qquad (98)$$

where c is the *velocity of sound* in water.

At $0°$ C, $c = 1403$ m/sec. The value in air at $0°$ C is 332 m/sec. This dramatic difference in sound propagation speed in air and water, due to the density difference, is reflective of the much lower attenuation, and greater reach, of sound in water than in air, and hence the criticality with regard to subsurface detectability.

For spherical waves with only a radial spatial dependence, as produced by the point sources, equation (98) reduces to

$$\frac{\partial^2 (rp)}{\partial t^2} = c^2 \frac{\partial^2 (rp)}{\partial r^2} \qquad (99)$$

A general form of the solution to equation (99), in view of the linearity of the equation and the Fourier series representation of the source disturbance, is

$$p = \frac{1}{r} \text{Re} \sum_{n=1}^{\infty} A_n e^{-in\omega(t-\frac{r}{c})} \qquad (100)$$

$\omega \equiv -N\Omega$ in equation (100), with the A_n being a set of constants to be determined. Equation (100) can also be written in the alternative forms

$$p = \frac{1}{r} \text{Re} \sum_{n=1}^{\infty} A_n e^{-i(n\omega t - \frac{2\pi r}{\lambda_n})}$$

or

$$p = \frac{1}{r} \text{Re} \sum_{n=1}^{\infty} A_n e^{-i(n\omega t - k_n r)} \qquad (101)$$

$\lambda_n \equiv 2\pi c/n\omega$ and $k_n \equiv n\omega/c = 2\pi/\lambda_n$ in equation (101) are the *acoustic wavelength* and *acoustic wave number*, respectively.

The exponential in equations (100) and (101) clearly identifies sound waves of different lengths, λ_n, but all traveling at the same speed. Zero value of the exponential argument in equation (100) implies an observer advancing at the speed of the wave system; the instantaneous position of the observer is $r = ct$, from the form of equation (100).

It is necessary to relate the A_n constants in the solution (100), (101) to the cavity volume velocity harmonics in equation (97). For this purpose, it is necessary to recognize that the governing equation is an alternative statement of Newton's Law applied to the radially expanding particles

$$-\frac{\partial p}{\partial r} = \rho \frac{\partial^2 \delta}{\partial t^2} \qquad (102)$$

where ρ is the (constant) water density and δ is the particle radial displacement on spherical surfaces.

Integration of equation (102) in time gives the normal (radial) particle velocity

$$v_r \equiv \frac{\partial \delta}{\partial t} = -\frac{1}{\rho} \int \frac{\partial p}{\partial r} dt \qquad (103)$$

Substitution of equation (101) produces

$$v_r = \frac{1}{\rho \omega} \frac{1}{r^2} \operatorname{Re} i \sum_{n=1}^{\infty} \frac{A_n}{n} \sqrt{1 + k_n^2 r^2} \cdot$$

$$\cdot e^{-i(n\omega t - k_n r + \tan^{-1} k_n r)} \qquad (104)$$

On the surface, $r = r_0(t)$, of the effective spherical cavity represented by the oscillating source, the radial velocity of the surface must equal the radial fluid velocity, v_r. The radial velocity of the surface is, by definition, just the instantaneous source strength divided by spherical surface area $4\pi r_0^2$. Equation (104) then becomes

$$\frac{Q(t)}{4\pi r_0^2} = \frac{1}{\rho \omega r_0^2} \operatorname{Re} i \sum_{n=1}^{\infty} \frac{A_n}{n} \sqrt{1 + k_n^2 r_0^2} \cdot$$

$$\cdot e^{-i(n\omega t - k_n r_0 + \tan^{-1} k_n r_0)} \qquad (105)$$

For $k_n r_0 = n\omega r_0 / c \ll 1$ on the scale of the far-field, equation (105) takes the limiting form:

$$\frac{Q(t)}{4\pi} = \frac{1}{\rho \omega} \operatorname{Re} i \sum_{n=1}^{\infty} \frac{A_n}{n} e^{-in\omega t} \qquad (106)$$

Now, substitute equation (97) and match terms on the two sides of equation (106) to obtain

$$A_n = -\frac{1}{4\pi} \rho i n N \omega \dot{\forall}_{nN} \qquad (107)$$

Back-substitution into equation (97) gives the solution of equation (98) for outgoing acoustic pressure waves generated by the periodically varying point source in its far-field

$$p(r,t) = -\frac{\rho N \omega}{4\pi r} \operatorname{Re} \sum_{n=1}^{\infty} i n \dot{\forall}_{nN} e^{-i(n\omega t - k_n r)} $$

or, for $\omega = -N\Omega$,

$$p(r,t) = \frac{\rho N^2 \Omega}{4\pi r} \operatorname{Re} \sum_{n=1}^{\infty} i n \dot{\forall}_{nN} e^{i(nN\Omega t - \frac{2\pi r}{\lambda_n})} \qquad (108)$$

Note from equation (108) that for $k_n r$ small, the sound pressure recovers the incompressible limit, which implies effectively infinite wave speed and instantaneous propagation over the small range of r/λ_n. This is the pressure involved in the near-field forces addressed in Section 2.3.

2.4.3 Far-Field Sound Intensity and Acoustic Power. Sound intensity, I, is defined as the average over a fundamental cycle of time of the sound power transmitted per unit area of the spherical surface. This is expressed as

$$I = \frac{1}{T} \int_0^T p v_r dt \qquad (109)$$

with the fundamental period $T = 2\pi/\omega$.

First, evaluate v_r by substitution of A_n from equation (107) into equation (104):

$$v_r = \frac{N}{4\pi r^2} \operatorname{Re} \sum_{n=1}^{\infty} \dot{\forall}_{nN} \sqrt{1 + k_n^2 r^2} \cdot$$

$$\cdot e^{-i(n\omega t - k_n r + \tan^{-1} k_n r)} \qquad (110)$$

Write v_r in a proper form for multiplication with p as

$$v_r = \frac{N}{8\pi r^2} \sum_{m=1}^{\infty} \kappa_m \left[\dot{\forall}_{mN} e^{-i(m\omega t - K_m)} + \right.$$

$$\left. + \overline{\dot{\forall}}_{mN} e^{i(m\omega t - K_m)} \right] \qquad (111)$$

with the overbar again denoting complex conjugate, and

$$\kappa_m \equiv \sqrt{1 + k_m^2 r^2} , \quad K_m \equiv k_m r - \tan^{-1} k_m r .$$

Substitute equations (108) and (111) into equation (109)

$$I = -\frac{\rho N^2 \omega}{32\pi^2 r^3} \frac{1}{T} \operatorname{Re} \sum_{n=1}^{\infty} \sum_{m=1}^{\infty} i n \kappa_m e^{ik_n r} \int_{t=0}^{T} \cdot$$

$$\cdot \left[\dot{\forall}_{mN} \dot{\forall}_{nN} e^{iK_m} e^{-i(n+m)\omega t} + \right.$$

$$\left. + \overline{\dot{\forall}}_{mN} \dot{\forall}_{nN} e^{-iK_m} e^{-i(n-m)\omega t} \right] dt \qquad (112)$$

The time integral in equation (112) is zero, by orthogonality, except when $m = n$ in the second term within the integral. The result is then

$$I = -\frac{\rho N^2 \omega}{32\pi^2 r^3} \operatorname{Re} \sum_{n=1}^{\infty} i n \kappa_n e^{-i \tan^{-1} k_n r} \dot{\forall}_{nN} \overline{\dot{\forall}}_{nN} \qquad (113)$$

The *acoustic power*, W, at any r, being the total acoustic power transmitted across the sphere of radius r, is then just the sound intensity times the spherical area

$$W = 4\pi r^2 I \qquad (114)$$

In consideration of I and W by equations (113) and (114), it can be observed that the product of the $\dot{\forall}_{nN}$ terms, being conjugates, is positive real and is the sum of the squares of the real and imaginary parts of $\dot{\forall}_{nN}$. Both I and W can therefore be written as pure real and positive

$$I = \frac{\rho N^3 \Omega}{32\pi^2 r^3} \sum_{n=1}^{\infty} n \kappa_n \sin(\tan^{-1} k_n r) \dot{\forall}_{nN} \overline{\dot{\forall}}_{nN} \qquad (115)$$

But with $\kappa_n = \sqrt{1 + k_n^2 r^2}$, equation (115) simplifies to

$$I = \frac{\rho N^3 \Omega}{32\pi^2 r^2} \sum_{n=1}^{\infty} n k_n \dot{\forall}_{nN} \overline{\dot{\forall}}_{nN} \qquad (116)$$

with

$$W = \frac{\rho N^3 \Omega}{8\pi} \sum_{n=1}^{\infty} n k_n \dot{\forall}_{nN} \overline{\dot{\forall}}_{nN} \qquad (117)$$

The back-substitution $\omega = -N\Omega$ is also included in equations (116) and (117).

These forms confirm that the acoustic power transmitted across a spherical surface of arbitrary radius is independent of the radius. This is necessary with no inclusion of acoustic damping in the governing wave equation, equation (98). W, by equation (117), is considered to be the acoustic power of the sound source.

2.4.4 Decibel Scaling. Because of the wide variation in acoustic quantities, it is standard to use a scale to reduce variability of the presented data; this is the *dB scale*, which expresses the acoustic quantities nondimensionally in terms of logarithms. But the constants of the log scaling differ for the different quantities (power, intensity, pressure), adjusted so that all fall numerically in the same compressed number range.

2.4.4.1 DECIBEL SCALE FOR POWER, *W*.   Sound power level (PWL) is expressed as

$$\text{PWL} = 10 \log_{10}(W/W_{ref}) \text{ dB} \qquad (118)$$

According to Beranek (1960), the line of thinking here is that if the reference power $W_{ref} = 1$ watt, and $W = 10$ watts, then PWL = 10 dB[1] since the $\log_{10}(10/1) = 1$. However, in consideration of desirable numerical ranges of scaling, the W_{ref} that is now used for acoustic power level specification for underwater noise is $W_{ref} = 10^{-13}$ watts.

---

[1]The term "level" is used exclusively in acoustics to denote the logarithmic dB scale.

From equation (118), with this reference power, and W in watts:

$$\text{PWL} = 10\log_{10}(W) + 130 \text{ dB} \qquad (119)$$

This scaling generally places marine acoustic noise power levels in the 50 to 150 dB range.

With *intensity*, equation (113), the reference scaling is conventionally $I_{ref} = 10^{-12}$ for I in watts/m², so that

$$\text{IL} = 10 \log_{10}(I) + 120 \text{ dB} \qquad (120)$$

For sound pressure, there is an additional consideration. Power and intensity are both positive quantities and both depend on sound pressure squared, so that the log in equations (119) and (120) is well defined. Pressure due to the oscillating source is both positive and negative with time. Taking the log of a negative number, which is undefined, is avoided by squaring the pressure:

$$\text{SPL} = 10 \log_{10}(p/p_{ref})^2$$

$$\equiv 20\log_{10}\left(\frac{|p|}{p_{ref}}\right) \qquad (121)$$

The convenient reference pressure here for marine acoustics pressure levels expected is $p_{ref} = 0.0002$ microbars. This is also considered to be the pressure amplitude threshold for hearing (Beranek, 1960, Chapter 3). With a microbar = 1 dyne/cm² = 1 standard barometric pressure (1 bar) × 10^{-6}, equation (121) therefore becomes, with p in microbars,

$$\text{SPL} = 20\log_{10}\left(\frac{|p|}{p_{ref}}\right)$$

$$= 20\log_{10}(|p|) + 74 \text{ dB} \qquad (122)$$

The uncertainty for application of equations (98) through (122) is the cavitation volume velocity harmonic set, $\dot{\forall}_q$. This was discussed more qualitatively in the last section. The limited cavity volume velocity data available is used in a specific example of underwater sound propagation in Section 3.

3
Analysis and Design

3.1 Introduction.   More and more over the years, ship designers are being faced with the requirement to deal effectively with propeller and machinery-induced vibration in design work. The uninitiated may feel uncomfortable, if not bewildered, by the seemingly endless complexity of the problem and the myriad of physical interrelationships influencing the required decisions.

Indeed, a mere description, without accompanying quantitative analysis, presents an imposing problem. Excluding effects of the seaway, the ship hull is excited mechanically by rotating machinery systems and hy-

drodynamically by its propeller(s). These excitation sources are essentially periodic, but they are not, in general, simple harmonic (i.e., purely sinusoidal). Because of this, excitations also occur at all multiples of a fundamental exciting frequency associated with each excitation source. The strengths of the various excitations, and their *harmonics*, are often highly sensitive to the details of design and fabrication. Moderate propeller cavitation, for example, which may be acceptable in all other respects, can produce hull vibratory excitation forces on the order of tens of tons, persistent at frequencies out to several multiples of the blade-rate fundamental (RPM times number of blades).

The infinity of excitations stimulate the ship to vibrate in generally all directions. The degree to which the ship responds is sensitive to its natural vibration characteristics or natural vibratory modes. Coincidence of the natural frequency identified with some natural mode and the exciting frequency of some excitation component corresponds to a condition of resonance. At resonance, rigidity is counterbalanced by inertia, and limitless vibratory amplification by the excitation is opposed only by damping, to first order. Since in ships, as in most engineering structures, damping is small, resonance is in general a condition that would be desirable to avoid.

Unfortunately, resonances cannot be avoided. The infinity of excitation frequencies overlies an even more dense infinity of natural frequencies. The natural modes vary in character from the overall lateral bending, axial, and torsional modes of the hull girder to highly localized vibration of plating panels, piping, handrails, and a plethora of others. Transmission paths of the vibration through the ship structure are highly influenced by distributions of local resonances, or near resonances; impedance to vibration transmission is reduced in regions where local resonances occur, and vice versa. The propagation of low-level, generally nonresonant vibration through a ship provides the base excitation capable of resonating local elements; this can often be observed in regions far removed from the source of the responsible excitation. The seeming complexity of it all is amplified upon recognition of the existence of dynamic as well as static coupling; excitations occurring in one direction can produce resonant vibration in other directions through the directional coupling of intervening structure. Substructures, or subregions, of a vessel that are treated as independent of one another in more conventional design considerations can be dynamically coupled to a significant degree. For example, longitudinal resonance in the main propulsion system can produce foundation dynamic forces and moments large enough to excite objectionable fore-and-aft rocking/bending of the vessel deckhouse, depending on the compliance of the intervening structure.

It is fortunate, in view of the above limitless latticework of unavoidable resonances, that, as frequency level increases, the various series of excitation harmonics do converge, the relevant natural vibratory modes become more difficult to excite, and the predominant damping mechanisms increase in strength.

Ship vibration is, in practice, not as difficult to deal with as the preceding description might suggest. With patience, the complexities can be systematically sorted out, more or less understood, and dealt with in a reasonably effective way through the basic vehicle of rational mechanics. Indeed, the general response formulas developed in the preceding section, equations (41) or (82), contain the near totality of possibilities for influencing

any vibration. These formulas predict the vibratory displacement of continuous (equation [41]), or discrete (equation [82]) mathematical models of vibratory systems. In either case, the system displacement is written as a superposition of displacements of a set of equivalent one-mass systems. The mass, stiffness, damping, and excitation force elements of each of the equivalent one-mass systems are constructed as explained in Section 2. The vibratory behavior of any complex system can therefore be dealt with in terms of the collection of equivalent one-mass systems vibrating simultaneously. For this reason, much insight into the various sensitivities of the vibration of any particular system, whether simple or complex, can be gained by applying a few simple observations from the theory for one-mass systems.

3.1.1 Basic Considerations. The general one-mass system is depicted in Fig. 15. The M, K, and C denote the mass, stiffness, and damping of the system, respectively, and $f(t)$ is the simple harmonic exciting force of amplitude F and frequency ω. The values of M, K, C, and F can be considered as independent of time, but vary, in general, with the exciting frequency, ω.

Either of the general response formulas of Section 2, equation (41) or (82), reduces to the following simple formula on application to the Fig. 15 one-mass system.

$$x(t) = \frac{F/K}{\sqrt{\left(1-(\omega/\omega_n)^2\right)^2 + (2\zeta\,\omega/\omega_n)^2}} \cos(\omega t - \alpha)$$
$$= X\cos(\omega t - \alpha) \qquad (123)$$

Here, X is the amplitude of the steady-state simple harmonic vibration displacement at frequency ω, and α is the displacement phase angle relative *to* $f(t)$

$$\alpha = \tan^{-1}\frac{2\zeta\,\omega/\omega_n}{1-(\omega/\omega_n)^2} \qquad (124)$$

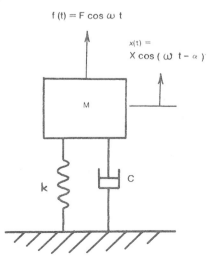

f (t) = F cos ω t

x(t) = X cos (ω t − α)

M

k   C

Fig. 15 Steady-state harmonic vibration of one-mass system.

By equations (74) and (80), the ω_n and ζ in equations (118) and (119) are

$$\omega_n = \sqrt{K/M} \qquad natural\ frequency$$
$$\zeta = C/2M\omega_n \qquad damping\ factor \qquad (125)$$

When considered in light of the general response formula, equation (82), the one-mass system displacement $x(t)$, can, by equation (123), be alternatively viewed as the contribution of one of the set of system modes to the complete system vibration. In this view, the M, K, C, and F are the *modal* values whose magnitudes vary from mode to mode depending on the distributions of system mass, stiffness, damping, and excitation relative to the *mode shape* of the particular mode; this is according to equations (73) through (78) of Section 2.

Figure 16 is the familiar plot of $X/(F/K)$ and α from equations (123) and (124) versus frequency ratio, ω/ω_n. Note that the function F/K is the vibratory displacement amplitude that would be predicted by quasistatic analysis. $X/(F/K)$ can therefore be viewed as a correction factor on the quasistatic displacement for dynamic effects. This ratio is called the dynamic *magnification factor*. It is apparent from Fig. 16 that the magnification factor can act to reduce the quasistatic displacement amplitude as well as to magnify it.

While Fig. 16 displays the basic character of the one-mass system vibration of interest, some care must be exercised in its interpretation. As noted, the M, C, K, and F are frequency dependent, in general. The curves of Fig. 16 can therefore be misleading with regard to the variation of vibratory amplitude and phase angle with frequency. For example, for an exciting force amplitude increasing as ω^2, such as in the case of a rotating machinery unbalance, multiplication of the Fig. 16 response characteristic with ω^2 is required in order to represent the correct frequency dependence of the actual displacement.

The Fig. 16 curves are instructive. However, the possibilities for influencing vibration are most directly apparent from formula (123) for one-mass system response. All possibilities lie in only four variables:

1. Excitation, F
2. Stiffness, K
3. Frequency ratio, ω/ω_n
4. Damping, ζ

It is obvious from equation (123) that any of the following contribute to vibration reduction.

1. Reduce exciting force amplitude, F. In propeller-induced ship vibration, the excitation is reduced by changing the propeller unsteady hydrodynamics. This may involve lines or clearance changes to reduce the nonuniformity of the wake inflow, or it may involve geometric changes to the propeller itself. Specifics in this regard are identified in the section on propeller excitation.

2. Increase stiffness, K. Stiffness, which is defined as spring force per unit static deflection, cannot be considered independently of frequency ratio, ω/ω_n, since $K = \omega_n^2 M$. However, equation (123) shows that stiffness should be increased rather than decreased when variations in natural frequency are to be accomplished by variations in stiffness. It is bad practice, in general, to reduce system stiffness in attempts to reduce vibration.

3. Avoid values of frequency ratio near unity; $\omega/\omega_n = 1$ is the resonant condition. From equation (123) at resonance

$$X = (F/K)/2\zeta \qquad (126)$$

Here, the excitation is opposed only by damping; note the peak in the frequency response curve of Fig. 16 at resonance. Obviously, ω/ω_n can be varied by varying either ω or ω_n. The spectrum of ω can be changed by changing the RPM of a relevant rotating machinery source, or, in the case of propeller-induced vibration, by changing the propeller RPM or its number of blades. ω_n is changed by changes in system mass and/or stiffness, by equation (125); increasing stiffness is the usual and preferred approach. Specific measures for resonance avoidance in ships are considered in the next section.

4. Increase damping, ζ. Damping of structural systems in general, and of ships in particular, is small; $\zeta < 1$. Therefore, except very near resonance, the vibratory amplitude is approximately

$$X = \frac{F/K}{\left| 1 - \left(\omega/\omega_n \right)^2 \right|}$$

which is damping independent. Damping is therefore relatively unimportant except in resonant vibration, by equation (126). Furthermore, damping is difficult to increase significantly in systems such as ships; ζ is the least effective of the four parameters available to the designer for implementing changes in ship vibratory characteristics.

3.1.2 Recommended Design Approach. While the basic vibratory behavior of ships is described qualitatively by the simple one-mass system formula, im-

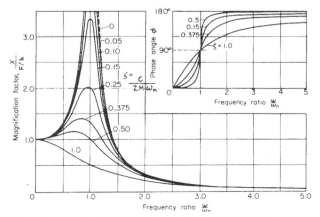

Fig. 16 Vibration response characteristic, one-mass system.

plementation of more general formulas, such as equation (82), is necessary if attempts at detailed quantification of ship vibratory response are to be made. However, it is widely accepted that the present state-of-the-art does not provide accurate enough definition of all of the system parameters, principally damping, to make detailed calculations of ship vibration response worth the effort as a routine design exercise. The designer should keep in touch with continuing research developments that may affect this view.

Accurate beforehand prediction of ship vibration response for, say, comparison against established habitability criteria would be desirable. However, experience has proved that such is not only impossible but also unnecessary in designing ships with consistently acceptable vibration characteristics. Four elements and their relationship to vibration reduction were identified in the preceding as being influential in determining ship vibratory response. While quantification of all four elements is required in predicting vibratory response level, acceptable results can usually be achieved with reasonable effort by focusing attention in design on only two of the four elements and de-emphasizing the importance of vibration response calculations, except in special cases. The two of the four elements of crucial importance in equation (123) are excitation and frequency ratio. The achievement in design of two objectives with regard to these elements has proved to result in ships with consistently acceptable vibration characteristics:

1. Minimization of the dominant vibratory excitations within the normal constraints imposed by other design variables, and
2. Avoidance of resonances involving active participation of major subsystems in frequency ranges where the dominant excitations are strongest.

Fortunately, unlike vibration response, the excitation and frequency ratio elements involved in these objectives are predictable with reasonable reliability. Detailed hydrodynamic calculation procedures in conjunction with model testing have been established in excitation analysis, at least to the level of reliable relative predictions. Natural frequencies involving the ship hull and its major subsystems are predictable using judicious modeling and modern numerical structural analysis methods. Hence, the accuracy levels achievable in predictions of propeller and engine excitation and of ship natural frequencies have been found to be high enough to consistently achieve the two objectives cited above. Approximate methods are discussed subsequently.

The detailed calculations and experiments required in assuring excitation minimization and resonance avoidance are usually performed by specialist groups or model basins, and are usually not the immediate responsibility of the ship designer. A main function of the ship designer in this regard is, however, to establish a concept or preliminary design to serve as the subject of the detailed investigations. The quality of the prelimi-

nary design will be reflected in the number of detailed iterations required for achieving an acceptable final design. For the purpose of establishing high-quality preliminary designs, which require a minimum of expensive and time-consuming calculations and model testing, the designer is desirous both of guidance as to the areas of his design likely to be in most need of attention and of some simple methodology for identifying the critical areas. As suggested by Johannessen and Skaar (1980), attention to vibration in preliminary design of large ships can usually be limited to the following main items.

1. Hull girder vertical vibration excited by a diesel main engine
2. Main machinery longitudinal vibration excited by the propeller
3. Superstructure longitudinal vibration excited by hull girder vertical vibration and/or main machinery longitudinal vibration

Many good sources are available for seeking help in resonance avoidance and excitation minimization with regard to these three critical items (American Bureau of Shipping, 2006; Bourceau & Voley, 1970; Breslin, 1970; Bureau Veritas, 1979; Johannessen & Skaar, 1980; Ward, 1982). The remainder of this section is directed specifically to the same need; the focus is on providing additional insight into, and facility in using, methodology of established effectiveness for approximate estimates of natural frequencies and exciting force levels for the three critical items cited above.

3.2 Approximate Evaluation of Hull Girder Natural Frequencies. The vertical beamlike modes of vibration of the hull girders of modern ships are dangerous in two respects:

1. They can be excited to objectionable levels by resonances with the dominant low-frequency excitations of low-RPM diesel main engines.
2. Vertical vibration of the hull girder in response to propeller excitation is a direct exciter of objectionable fore-and-aft superstructure vibration.

The propeller is generally incapable of exciting the hull girder modes to dangerous levels. This is primarily because the higher hull girder modes, whose natural frequencies fall in the range where propeller excitation is significant, have low excitability (refer to the discussion of Fig. 5 in Section 2). However, the low-level vertical hull girder vibration that does occur serves as the base excitation for excessive vibration of superstructures and other attached subsystems that are in resonance with the propeller exciting frequencies. The mechanics of this excitation is demonstrated by the base-excited deckhouse example of Section 2.

The natural frequencies corresponding to the two-noded vertical bending modes of conventional ship hulls can be estimated with reasonable accuracy using either the Burrill (1934–1935) or the Todd (1961) formula, of which the latter can take account of the effect of long superstructures. A later formulation was given by Kumai (1968). Kumai's formula for two-noded vertical bending is

$$N_{2v} = 3.07 \cdot 10^6 \sqrt{\frac{I_v}{\Delta_i L^3}} \quad cpm \tag{127}$$

where

I_v = moment of inertia (m⁴)

$$\Delta_i = \left(1.2 + \frac{1}{3} \cdot \frac{B}{T_m}\right)\Delta$$

Δ = displacement, including virtual added mass of water (tons)

L = length between perpendiculars (m)

B = breadth amidships (m)

T_m = mean draft (m)

Table 1, from Johannessen and Skaar (1980), gives an indication of the accuracy that can be expected from equation (127). The table compares the prediction of the two-noded vertical hull bending natural frequency by Kumai's formula with the predictions of detailed finite element calculations performed on seven different ships.

The two-noded hull vertical bending natural frequencies actually lie well below the dangerous exciting frequencies of either typical diesel main engines or propellers, and are therefore of little consequence in these considerations. As will be demonstrated further on, it is hull girder modes with typically a minimum of four or five nodes that can be excited excessively by the diesel main engine. In the case of the propeller, the hull girder vertical bending modes that fall near full-power propeller blade-rate excitation are typically more than seven-noded. Full-power blade-rate excitation of large ships is usually in the range of 8 to 12 Hz; as indicated in Table 1, the two-noded vertical hull bending mode, on the order of 1 to 2 Hz, is well below the blade-rate excitation frequency level during normal operation.

It is observed that hull girder natural frequencies increase more or less linearly with node number from

the two-noded value for the first few modes. The data shown in Fig. 17, from Johannessen and Skaar (1980), provide estimates of the natural frequencies of the first four vertical bending modes of general cargo ships and of the first five vertical bending modes of tankers. Note the good agreement between the Table 1 data and Fig. 17 for two-noded cases. Also, note that the 6 Hz maximums represented by Fig. 17 still lie well below typical

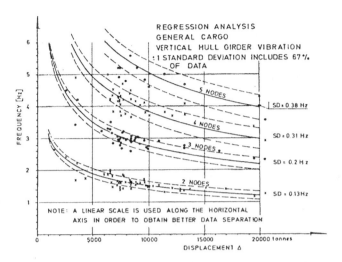

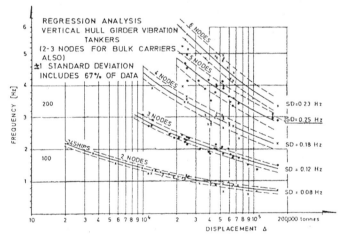

Fig. 17 Natural frequencies of vertical hull vibration.

Table 1   Comparison of Two-noded Hull Vertical Vibration Natural Frequencies, Hz

Ship Number	Type	Size (tons)	Kumai Method	Finite Element Method	Dev. %
1	reefer	15,000	1.54	1.51	+2
2	RO/RO	32,000	1.46	1.16	+26
3	RO/RO	49,000	1.49	1.6	−7
4	RO/RO	42,000	1.04	0.94	+10
5	chemical tanker	33,000	1	1	+8
6	bulk carrier	73,000	0.63	0.64	
7	multipurpose	15,500	2	1.62	+23

full-power propeller excitation frequencies, and the accuracy of the data fits indicated on the figure is deteriorating rapidly as modal order increases. The primary reason for the increasing data scatter with node number is the increasing influence of local effects (i.e., approaching resonances of deckhouses, decks, etc.) on the basic beam modes still identifiable.

The Kumai (1968) formula, in conjunction with Fig. 17, is, however, useful in preliminary steps to avoid resonances with a main diesel engine. The following formula, from Johannessen and Skaar (1980) and representing the Fig. 17 data, expresses the first few vertical bending natural frequencies in terms of the two-noded value.

$$N_{nv} \approx N_{2v}(n-1)^{\alpha} \qquad (128)$$

α = 0.845 general cargo ships
= 1.0 bulk carriers
= 1.02 tankers

Here N_{2v} is the two-noded vertical natural frequency and n is the number of nodes; n should not exceed 5 or 6 in order to remain within the range of reasonable validity of equation (128). Note the approximate proportionality of N_{nv} to node number in equation (128); this is also evident in Fig. 17.

More accurate estimates of the lower hull girder modes can be obtained by modeling the hull girder as a nonuniform beam. The basic model required is essentially that used in static calculations of longitudinal strength. The natural frequency analysis should therefore be within the capability of the conventional design office, which now routinely engages in computerized longitudinal strength calculations. The nonuniform beam dynamic analysis differs from the static analysis in one major respect, however. A hydrodynamic added mass distribution must be estimated and superimposed on the vessel mass distribution in order to obtain natural frequency estimates with any degree of realism. Estimation of the required added mass distribution for use in calculating the hull girder vertical modes by way of nonuniform beam analysis is the subject of the next subsection.

3.3 Hydrodynamic Added Mass. Ships are unlike most other vehicles because of the substantial inertial effects to which they are subjected by the high-density medium in which they operate. The water inertia forces, being proportional to ship surface accelerations, imply an equivalent, or effective, fluid mass, imagined to accelerate along with the ship mass. This effective mass is termed *hydrodynamic added mass*.

Hydrodynamic added mass is usually large. For example, in the case of a deeply submerged circular cylinder in heave motion, ideal fluid theory predicts an added mass per unit length of the cylinder equal to the mass per unit length of displaced fluid. The corresponding value for a sphere is one half the mass of the fluid displaced. Added mass effects cannot be ignored in ship vibration analysis.

The calculation method of Lewis (1929) currently remains the most popular method for estimating the added mass distribution of a vertically vibrating ship. By Lewis, the hydrodynamic added mass per unit length at longitudinal position x along the vertically vibrating ship is

$$m(x) = (\pi/8)\rho B^2(x)C(x)J_n \quad t/m \qquad (129)$$

where

ρ = density of water, t/m^3
$B(x)$ = section beam, m
$C(x)$ = section two-dimensional added mass coefficient
J_n = Lewis J-factor, representing a reduction factor on the two-dimensional added mass for three-dimensionality of the vibration-induced flow

The two-dimensional section added-mass coefficient, $C(x)$, is determined using the so-called *Lewis form* conformal mapping of the ship sections.

This transformation of the form

$$Z = z + \frac{a(x)}{z} + \frac{b(x)}{z^3} \qquad (130)$$

transforms a unit circle from the z plane into the ship section plane Z. The shape of the particular ship section is represented in equation (130) by the mapping parameters $a(x)$ and $b(x)$; $a(x)$ and $b(x)$ are determined so that the section area coefficient and beam/draft ratio are preserved in the transformation. On specification of a and b, the ideal fluid solution for the unit circle manipulates to give the two-dimensional added mass for the ship section. All of this is concisely represented in Fig. 18, which was constructed by Todd (1935). $C(x)$ can be extracted from Fig. 18 on specification of the section area coefficient, $A(x)/[B(x)T(x)]$, and the section beam/

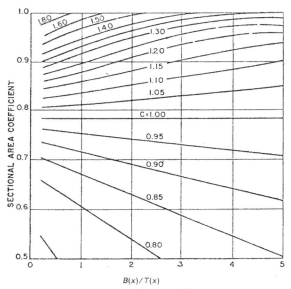

Fig. 18 Virtual-mass coefficients.

draft ratio. Typical Lewis form section shapes are shown in Beck and Reed (2010) on motions on waves.

The J-factor in equation (129) is most easily defined by rewriting the equation as

$$m(x) = m_{2-D}(x)J_n \qquad (131)$$

where

$$m_{2-D} = (\pi/8)\rho B^2 C \qquad (132)$$

m_{2-D} is the two-dimensional added mass per unit length at section x. Then, integrating equation (132) over the ship length,

$$M = J_n \int m_{2-D}(x)dx \equiv M_{2-D} J_n$$

gives

$$J_n = M/M_{2-D} \qquad (133)$$

where J_n is the ratio of the total added mass in n-noded vibration to the total value assuming two-dimensional flow, section by section.

Lewis assumed that this ratio, equation (133), for a ship was approximately equal to that for a spheroid (ellipse of revolution) of the same beam/length ratio. The exact theoretical value of M, as well as that of M_{2-D}, is available for the spheroid ideal fluid flow theory.

J_n so determined from the spheroid calculations (Vorus & Hylarides, 1981), can be extracted from Fig. 19;

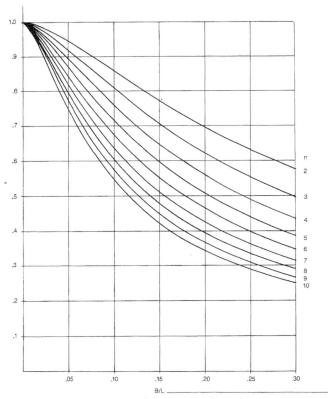

Fig. 19 Lewis J-factor (n is mode number).

B/L in Fig. 19 involves the midship beam, B, rather than the section beam, $B(x)$, used in Fig. 18. The J_n are functions of the number of nodes, n, in the hull girder vibration; the J_n, and therefore the added mass, varies mode by mode. Note from Fig. 19 that the J_n decreases with increasing n; this is due to the increasing three-dimensionality of the flow in the higher modes.

For example, consider a ship section with $A(x)/[B(x) T(x)] = 0.9$, $B(x)/T(x) = 2$, and $B/L = 0.15$. From Fig. 18, $C(x) = 1.17$. Assume that the seven-noded hull vertical natural frequency is of interest. For seven nodes, from Fig. 19, $J_7 = 0.515$.

With $\rho = 1$ t/m^3 for SW, the added mass per unit length at the section is, from equation (129),

$$m(x) = 0.237\, B^2 \quad \text{t/m}$$

3.4 Approximate Evaluation of Superstructure Natural Frequencies. With the movement of engine rooms and deckhouses aft over the propeller, propeller-induced vibration of stern-mounted superstructures became one of the naval architectís greatest concerns. As proposed in the preceding section, a nonuniform beam model that ignores the dynamics of sprung substructures produces useful estimates of the hull girder lower natural frequencies for purposes of resonance avoidance with a main diesel engine. It is indeed fortunate that the lower rocking/bending natural frequencies associated with stern superstructures, which usually fall in the range of propeller blade-rate exciting frequencies, can, conversely, be estimated with useful accuracy by ignoring the dynamics of the hull girder. This is the case when the mass of the superstructure is small relative to the effective mass of the hull girder near the coupled natural frequencies of interest. Any consideration of vibratory response versus natural frequencies alone must, on the other hand, allow for the dynamic coupling. This is clear considering the fact that, in the preponderance of cases, superstructure vibration is excited by the hull girder vibration at its base.

The superstructure vibration mode of primary concern is a fore-and-aft rocking/bending mode excited through vertical vibration of the hull girder; an idealization of this mode was developed for conceptual purposes in Section 2.1.

For obtaining preliminary estimates of superstructure fore-and-aft rocking/bending natural frequencies, the semiempirical method of Hirowatari and Matsumoto (1969) has proved to have great utility (Sandstrom & Smith, 1979). The Hirowatari method was developed from correlation of simple analysis and measured fore-and-aft superstructure natural frequencies on approximately 30 ships. In this method, the fore-and-aft "fixed-base" natural frequency of the superstructure (i.e., superstructure cantilevered from the main deck) is determined according to deckhouse type and height. The fixed-base natural frequency is then reduced by a correction factor to account for the rotational flexibility of the underdeck supporting structure. Specifically, the procedure of Hirowatari is as follows.

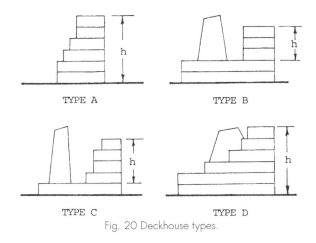

TYPE A   TYPE B

TYPE C   TYPE D

Fig. 20 Deckhouse types.

Table 2 Flexible Base Correction Factors

Type	f_e/f_∞
A,C	0.625
B	0.602
D	0.751

1. Select superstructure type from Fig. 20.
2. Determine superstructure height, h.
3. Read f_∞ (fixed-base natural frequency) as a function of h from Fig. 21.
4. Read f_e/f_∞ (the correction factor) from Table 2.
5. Compute f_e (the expected deckhouse natural frequency in the first fore-and-aft mode) from the following formula.

$$f_e = f_\infty (f_e/f_\infty) \qquad (134)$$

It is reported in Sandstrom and Smith (1979) that this procedure generally produces results that are within 15% of measurements from shaker tests. However, the method becomes inapplicable when the superstructure type varies significantly from those given in Fig. 20. Furthermore, there is some uncertainty regarding the use of the correction factors for superstructure support flexibility given in Table 2, since the supporting structure may vary from deep beams to column supports to structural bulkheads. Despite these difficulties, the method seems to work quite well in most cases, considering the limited input that is required. This feature makes the Hirowatari method particularly attractive in the early design stages when the design data are sparse or unknown.

In either design studies or in postdesign corrective investigations, the best approach is often to develop, or to calibrate, a mathematical model from which to evaluate the effects of design changes. Proceeding with the idea of approximations using simple analysis, the two basic effects influencing the fundamental fore-and-aft superstructure natural frequency are exemplified in Hirowatari's approach:

1. Cantilever (fixed-base) bending and shear of the superstructure as a beam over its height h (see Fig. 21)
2. Rocking of the superstructure as a rigid box on the effective torsional stiffness of its supporting structure

Ordinarily, one of the superstructure main transverse bulkheads will be a continuation of one of the two engine room transverse bulkheads. The intersection of the continuous bulkhead and the deck identified with the superstructure base (see Fig. 20) can usually be taken as the axis about which the rocking of the house occurs.

The fore-and-aft natural frequency of the superstructure due to the combined effects of rocking and bending/shear can be estimated using Dunkerley's equation (Thomson, 1973) as

$$f_e = \sqrt{\frac{1}{1/f_\infty{}^2 + 1/f_R{}^2}} \qquad (135)$$

Here, f_∞ has been identified as the fixed base cantilever natural frequency, from Fig. 21, or by analysis. f_R in equation (135) is the rocking natural frequency of the rigid superstructure, of height h, on its supporting stiffness

$$f_R = 60/2\pi \sqrt{K_f / J} \; cpm \qquad (136)$$

J is the mass moment of inertia of the superstructure about the rocking axis, and K_f is the effective torsional stiffness of the superstructure foundation, also about the axis of rotation.

The Hirowatari procedure, in conjunction with equations (135) and (136), has utility in design or postdesign corrective studies where estimates must be made as to the relative effects of structural changes. This is demonstrated by the numerical example that follows:

Assume that a conventional Type A superstructure (see Fig. 20) has been preliminarily designed. The house height, h, is 16 m. Referring to Figs. 20 and 21 and Table 1,

$$f_\infty = 750 \; cpm$$

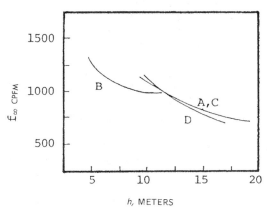

Fig. 21 Fixed base superstructure natural frequencies.

and

$$f_e/f_\infty = 0.625$$

which gives the estimated fore-and-aft house natural frequency, f_e, as

$$f_e = 0.625(750) = 469 \; cpm$$

The rocking frequency is estimated from equation (135) as

$$f_R = \sqrt{\frac{1}{1/f_e^2 - 1/f_\infty^2}} = 601 \; cpm$$

From equation (136) then,

$$K_f/J = (2\pi/60)^2 f_R^2 = 3961 \; rad^2/sec^2 \qquad (137)$$

Now assume that the mass of the house, m, has been estimated as 300 tons. Also assume that the house front is a continuation of the engine room forward transverse bulkhead, so that the house effectively rotates about its front lower edge (Fig. 22). Assume a radius of gyration, $\bar{r}$, of the house about this axis of 10 m. The house mass moment of inertia, J, is then

$$J = m\bar{r}^2 = 3 \times 10^7 \; kg - m^2$$

The effective rotational stiffness of the foundation is then estimated from equation (137) as

$$K_f = 1.19 \times 10^{11} N - m/rad \qquad (138)$$

Proceeding with the scenario, assume that stiffening is proposed in the form of two parallel pillars made up of 20 cm extra-heavy steel pipe, each 6 m long, and located under the house side bulkheads as indicated in Fig. 22.

The effective axial stiffness of the parallel pillars, allowing serial stiffness of the structure at the pipe connections, is calculated to be

$$k = 4 \times 10^8 \; N/m$$

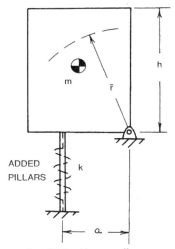

Fig. 22 Deckhouse stiffening.

The pillars are located at a distance $a = 6$ m aft of the forward bulkhead, so that the incremental rotational stiffness added by the pillars is

$$\delta K_f = ka^2 = 1.44 \times 10^{10} \; N - m/rad$$

The stiffness of the stiffened foundation is, in view of equation (138),

$$K_f' = K_f + \delta K_f = 1.334 \times 10^{11} \; N - m/rad$$

which represents a 12.1% increase. The new rocking frequency, from equation (136), becomes

$$f_R' = f_R\sqrt{1.121} = 636 \; cpm$$

Then, from equation (137), the house fore-and-aft natural frequency is raised to

$$f_e' = \sqrt{\frac{1}{1/f_\infty^2 + 1/f_R^2}} = 485 \; cpm$$

which represents a 3.4% increase over the value of 469 cpm without the pillars.

The simple analysis in this example should have been at least useful for judging that the proposed pillars would not be very effective in raising the superstructure natural frequency.

3.5 Main Thrust Bearing Foundation Stiffness. This subject has been a naval architecture responsibility very important to longitudinal vibration of main propulsion machinery, which is the second critical subject identified in Section 3.1. However, with the shift to almost universal use of diesel main engines for commercial vessels, the mounting length of the engine itself provides inherently greater stiffness than tended to occur with steam plants. That is, the length of the diesel engine reduces the opportunity for rocking/bending on the spring of the double bottom structure. This subject is therefore removed from the critical list for treatment here, and the reader is referred to Harrington (1992).

3.6 Diesel Engine Excitation. Diesel engine vibratory excitation can be generally considered as composed of three periodic force components and three periodic moment components acting at the engine foundation. Actually, the periodic force component along the axis of the engine is inherently zero, and some other components usually balance to zero depending on particular engine characteristics.

Two distinctly different types of forces can be associated with the internal combustion reciprocating engine: (a) gas pressure forces due to the combustion processes, and (b) inertia forces produced by the accelerations of the reciprocating and rotating engine parts.

As shown by Den Hartog (1956), the gas pressures can produce only torsional moments about the engine fore-and-aft axis; the vertical and transverse gas pressure forces balance within the engine and, assuming engine rigidity, do not appear at the foundation. The vertical force and moment, which are of primary concern with regard to hull vibratory excitation, and the transverse force and moment as well, are due entirely to unbalanced inertial effects. But following the Den Hartog analysis, it is readily seen that for engines of more than two cylinders, which is the case of interest with ships, the vertical and transverse inertia force components also balance identically to zero at the engine foundation. This leaves only the vertical and transverse moments about which to be concerned. These moments can be written as

$$m_y(t) = \mathrm{Re}M_{y1}e^{i\Omega t} + \mathrm{Re}M_{y2}e^{2i\Omega t} \qquad (139)$$

and:

$$m_z(t) = \mathrm{Im}M_{z1}e^{i\Omega t}$$

Here, m_y is the vertical moment about the transverse y axis (Fig. 23), and m_z is the transverse moment about the vertical z axis. Ω in equation (139) is the engine angular velocity, in radians per second.

The complex notation in equation (139) is for convenience in defining the moment amplitudes. By definition

$$e^{ix} \equiv \cos x + i\sin x$$

where i = $\sqrt{-1}$.

The Re and Im in equation (139) imply the use of only the real or imaginary part, respectively, of the complex numbers formed from the products of the complex moment amplitudes and the complex exponentials.

Equation (139) shows that the vertical moment, m_y, has both once-per-revolution and twice-per-revolution

components; the transverse moment occurs exclusively at the once-per-revolution engine RPM frequency.

The complex moment amplitudes in equation (139) are given by the following formulas.

$$M_{y1} = (M_{rec} + M_{rot})r\Omega^2\ell_c\sum_{m=1}^{M}me\,\frac{2\pi i(k_m-1)}{M}$$

$$M_{y2} = M_{rec}\frac{r^2}{\ell}\Omega^2\ell_c\sum_{m=1}^{M}me\,\frac{4\pi i(k_m-1)}{M}$$

$$M_{z1} = M_{rot}\,r\,\Omega^2\ell_c\sum_{m=1}^{M}me\,\frac{2\pi i(k_m-1)}{M} \qquad (140)$$

The variables in equation (140) are, with the aid of Fig. 23,

• M_{rec} and M_{rot} represent the equivalent masses experiencing the accelerations of the piston and crank pin, respectively, of one cylinder, due to the constant crankshaft angular velocity Ω. The mass M_{rec} is composed of the mass of the piston assembly and piston rod, plus a fraction of the mass of the connecting rod. The mass M_{rot} is composed of the balance of the connecting rod mass, plus an equivalent mass at the crank pin representing the weight eccentricity of the crank throw.

• r is the crank radius, ℓ is the connecting rod length, ℓ_c is the longitudinal distance between the cylinder axes, M is the number of cylinders, and k_m is the firing order of the mth cylinder; for $m = 1, \ldots M$, k_m has generally nonconsecutive integer values $1, \ldots, M$.

The real amplitudes of the moment components, which correspond to the maximum values of interest, are just the respective moduli of equation (140). The values of the moment amplitudes are usually tabulated in the manual for a particular engine. They can also be calculated by equation (140). This is demonstrated by the following example.

The majority of low speed marine diesels currently in service have six cylinders. A typical firing order for such engines is 1-5-3-4-2-6. With $M = 6$ and $k_m = 1, 5, 3, 4, 2, 6$ for $m = 1, \ldots, 6$, the summations in equation (140) are

$$\sum_{m=1}^{M}me\,\frac{2\pi i(k_m-1)}{M} = 0$$

and

$$\sum_{m=1}^{M}me\,\frac{4\pi i(k_m-1)}{M} = 3 - 1.732i$$

The foundation moment amplitudes are therefore:

$$M_{y1} = 0$$

$$M_{y2} = -M_{rec}(r^2/\ell)\Omega^2\ell_c(3 + 1.732i) \quad M_{z1} = 0$$

This shows that in the case of the six-cylinder engine of the above firing order, only the second-order vertical moment, aside from a torsion, exists to excite the hull. The magnitude of this moment, usually denoted as M, is

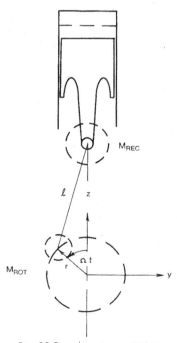

Fig. 23 Diesel engine excitation.

$$M_{2v} = \left| M_{y2} \right| = 3.464 \, M_{rec} \left(r^2 / \ell \right) \Omega^2 \ell_c \qquad (141)$$

Data for the Sulzer RND 76M engine, from Sulzer Bros. (1977), is

Stroke: $2r$	1.55 m
Connecting rod length, ℓ	3.775 m
and mass,	3.22 tons
Mass of piston, piston rod,	
and cross-head	4.76 tons
Crankshaft length	9.6 m
RPM	122

Taking one half of the connecting rod mass as effective in reciprocating with the piston, the data for use with equation (140) are

$$M_{rec} = 6.37$$
$$r = 0.775$$
$$\ell = 3.775 \text{ m}$$
$$\Omega = 122 \, (2\pi/60) = 12.78 \text{ rad/sec}$$
$$\ell_c = 9.6/5 = 1.92 \text{ m}$$

Substitution of the data into equation (141) gives

$$M_{2v} = 112.3 \text{ t-m}$$

The value from the data book for this engine is 119.4 t-m.

The second-order vertical moment of this example is the diesel engine excitation of most concern; it is larger than the first-order moments, in general. One guideline (Johannessen & Skaar, 1980) recommends attention in cases where M_{2v} exceeds 50 t-m. The potential danger is in resonating one of the lower hull girder vertical modes with a large second-order vertical moment. This possibility is demonstrated by the following example.

Table 1 in Section 3.2 gives estimated values for the fundamental two-noded vertical hull critical for a number of different ships. Section 3.2 also suggests a simple extrapolation equation (128) for estimating the first few higher-mode natural frequencies, given the fundamental value

$$N_{nv} \approx N_{2v} \quad (n - 1)^\alpha \, (n \text{ not to exceed } \sim 5)$$

Assuming the "reefer," ship number 1 of Table 1, for example, $N_{2v} = 92.4$ cpm, and $\alpha = 0.845$. The first four vertical hull-girder modes of this vessel would then be predicted to have corresponding natural frequencies of

$n = N$ (cpm)
2 = 92.4
3 = 166
4 = 234
5 = 298

The frequency of the second-order engine excitation from the previous example is $2 \times$ RPM = 244 cpm. It is relatively close to the predicted natural frequency of the four-noded third hull girder mode.

While the natural frequency estimate of 234 cpm is indeed rough, it should at least have been reliable enough to dictate further analysis to refine the hull girder natural frequency estimates in this particular example.

In the case of projected high excitability in resonant vibration with the diesel engine moments, which does develop in the course of design on occasion, the excitation moment components can usually be reduced effectively by the incorporation of compensators (Sulzer Bros., 1977). These devices consist of rotating counterweights usually geared directly to the engine crank. They are rotated at the proper rate and with the proper phase to produce cancellation with the undesirable first- or second-order engine-generated moment.

An alternative that has seen increasing popularity with medium-speed engines is the installation of main diesel (x) engines on resilient mounts. Schlottmann et al. (1999, 2000a, 2000b) provided an introduction into the basics of resilient mounting and the models used for analysis. The question of whether to use rigid or flexible engine mountings is underlined by a project (Rubber Design BV, Deutz MWM) in which a rigid mounting installation was replaced by a flexible one via resilient mounts (Anonymous, 1997). Due to reportedly successful results, the owner altered a series of seven ships on the basis of his belief that isolating the main engine on resilient mounts was the best approach to minimizing hull vibration and structure-born noise.

3.7 Propeller Excitation. Propeller excitation is far more difficult to quantify than the excitation from internal machinery sources. This is because of the complexity of the unsteady hydrodynamics of the propeller operating in the nonuniform hull wake. In fact, the nonuniform hull wake is the most complicated part; it is unfortunate that it is also the most important part. Propeller-induced vibration would never be a consideration in ship design if the wake inflow to the propeller disk was circumferentially uniform. Any treatment of propeller excitation must begin with a consideration of the hull wake.

3.7.1 Hull Wake Characteristics. In reality, hull wakes are both time-varying and circumferentially nonuniform. Under steady-ahead operation, which is the condition of primary interest when ship vibration is the concern, time variations of the wake are entirely random variations associated with the random character of boundary layer turbulence and the seaway in which the ship operates. Random vibration analyses of ships are therefore implied. However, the present and forseeable technology allows for the circumferential nonuniformity of hull wakes, but assumes, for steady operation, that wake is time invariant in a ship-fixed coordinate system.

Although several empirical formulations have been proposed for estimating time average ship wake distributions (Holden, Fagerjold, & Ragnar, 1980), it is generally accepted at this time that model tests are required. The model nominal wake field, which is conventionally measured in the propeller disk by pitot tube survey with the propeller removed (Pien, 1958), is, however, not a completely accurate representation of the time average inflow. Both distortions of the rotational flow by the propeller and the diffraction flow component from the hull boundary are absent, and scaling is a problem. Efforts are usually made to apply corrections to model nominal wakes for these effects (Dyne, 1974; Huang & Groves, 1981; Sasajima & Tanaka, 1966). However, the uncorrected model nominal wakes are probably adequate for the relative types of evaluation often of primary interest in design studies.

Model nominal wake data are presented either as a contour plot or as curves of velocity versus angular position at different radii in the propeller disc. The latter representation for the axial and tangential velocity components for a conventional stern single screw merchant ship (Hadler & Cheng, 1965) is shown in Fig. 24; a radial component also exists, of course, but it has little influence on propeller vibratory forces.

The position angle, θ, in Fig. 24 is taken as positive counterclockwise, looking forward, and x is positive aft. The axial and tangential wake velocities in Fig. 24 are nondimensional on the ship forward speed, U.

Note from Fig. 24 that the axial velocity is symmetric in θ about top dead-center (even function) and the tangential velocity is asymmetric (odd function). This is a characteristic of single screw ships due to the transverse symmetry of the hull relative to the propeller disk; such

wake symmetry does not exist with twin-screw ships. Usually, velocities are measured only over the half-circles of the propeller disk in single screw cases, with opposite-hand projections on the basis of the required symmetry. Occasionally, the full circles are measured; the measured deviations from symmetry reflect the inaccuracies of model construction and instrumentation, as well as possible inconsistencies in obtaining true time averages.

The wake illustrated in Fig. 24 represents one of the two characteristically different types of single-screw ship wakes. The flow character of the conventional *cruiser* or *clearwater* stern in Fig. 24 is basically waterline flow; the streamlines are more or less horizontal along the skeg and into the propeller disk. The flow components along the steep buttock lines forward of the propeller disk are small. The dominant axial velocity field of the resultant wake has a substantial defect running vertically through the disk along its vertical centerline, at all radii. This defect is the shadow of the skeg immediately forward. The tangential flow in the propeller disk, being the component of the upward flow toward the free surface, is relatively small. The idealization of this wake is the two-dimensional flow behind an infinitely long vertical strut placed ahead of the propeller. In this idealization, the axial velocity distribution is invariant vertically, and the tangential (and radial) velocities are symmetric about the transverse disk axis. The basic character can be detected in the Fig. 24 data.

A characteristically different wake flow is that associated with the *strut* or *barge-type* stern, which has a broad counter above the propeller disk and little irregularity forward. The flow character over this type of stern is basically along the buttock lines, versus the waterlines. Some wake nonuniformity may be produced by appendages forward, such as struts and bearings, or by shaft inclination, but the main wake defect, depending on the relative disk position, will be that of the counter-boundary layer overhead. In this case, a substantial axial wake again exists but only in the top of the propeller disk. As generally only the blade tips penetrate the overhead boundary layer, the axial wake defect occurs only at the extreme radii near top dead-center, rather than at all radii along the vertical centerline, as in the characterization of the conventional single-screw stern. Just as in the case of the conventional stern, the tangential disk velocity with the strut stern will be generally small; the vertically upward velocity ratio through the propeller disk will have average values on the order of the tangent of the sum of the buttock and shaft inclination angles. The idealization in the case of the barge stern, as a sequel to the vertical strut idealization of the wake of the conventional stern, is an infinite horizontal flat plate above the propeller. Here, the degree of axial wake nonuniformity depends on the overlap between the propeller disk and the plate boundary layer. The tangential and radial wake components are due entirely to the shaft inclination angle in this idealization, as the flat-plate boundary layer produces only an axial defect.

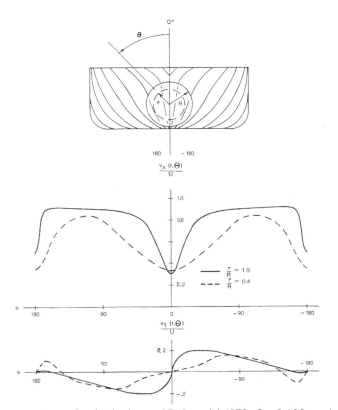

Fig. 24 Nominal wake distribution, DTMB model 4370, C_B =0.602, moderate V-stern.

3.7.1.1 PROPELLER/HULL CLEARANCE.   The distinction between the two different wake types is important to understanding the importance of clearances between the propeller blades and local hull surfaces. First of all, it is helpful to consider the hull surface excitation as composed of two effects:

Wake effect—The effect of changing the wake inflow to the propeller according to a specified propeller relocation but with the propeller actually fixed in position relative to the hull.

Diffraction effect—The effect of changing the propeller location relative to the hull but with the wake inflow to the propeller held fixed.

It is a common misconception that the cruciality of propeller/hull clearances has to do primarily with the diffraction effect. To the contrary, studies show that for wake inflow held invariant, propeller-induced excitation level is relatively insensitive to near-field variations in propeller location. It is the high sensitivity of propeller blade pressures and cavitation inception to the variations in wake nonuniformity accompanying clearance changes that dictate the need for clearance minima. In general, the wake gradients become more extreme as propeller/hull clearances are decreased.

Reconsider the conventional and strut-stern wake types in light of the above fact. It is probable that too much emphasis is often placed on aperture clearances in conventional stern single-screw ships. From the point of view of vertical clearance, there is no significant boundary layer on the narrow counter above the propeller with this stern type. Furthermore, from the point of view of the vertical strut idealization of the skeg, the axial velocity distribution would be invariant with vertical disk position. The critical item with vertical tip clearance in the conventional stern case seems to be the waterline slope in the upper skeg region. Blunt waterline endings can result in local separation and substantially more severe wake gradients in the upper disk than suggested by the strut idealization. Fore-and-aft clearances in the conventional stern case should be even less critical than the vertical clearances. Wakes attenuate very slowly with distance downstream. While increasing the fore-and-aft clearances between the blade tips and the skeg edge forward certainly acts to reduce the wake severity, the reduction will be marginally detectable within the usual limits of such clearance variation. An exception may exist in the case of separation in the upper disk due to local waterline bluntness. The closure region of the separation bubble exhibits relatively large gradients in axial velocity.

For the broad, flat-countered, strut-stern vessel, the vertical tip clearance is a much more critical consideration. A relatively uniform wake will result if the propeller disk does not overlap the overhead boundary layer. This is, in general, the condition achieved on naval combatant vessels; the rule of thumb in U.S. Naval design practice is a minimum vertical tip clearance of one quarter the propeller diameter. Vibration problems are almost unheard of on U.S. Naval combatants.

Some wake nonuniformity on strut-stern ships does result from shaft struts and from the relatively high shaft inclinations often required to maintain the 25% overhead tip clearances. With proper alignment to the flow, shaft struts produce highly localized irregularities in the wake that are generally not effective in the production of vibratory excitation. The main effect of shaft inclination is a relative upflow through the propeller disk. The cavitation that can result at the 3- and 9-o'clock blade positions has proved to be of concern with regard to noise and minor blade erosion, but the hull vibratory excitation produced has never been considered to be of significance.

The clearance minimum of 25% of a propeller diameter is more or less the standard in commercial practice as well as naval, although some classification rules show less. In conventional stern merchant ships, the vertical clearances tend to average slightly less (~0.15 D) and forward clearances from blade tips to skeg average slightly more (~0.3 D). Some conservatism exists in these rules of thumb, or they would not have withstood the test of time. However, the studies needed to provide a rationale for clearance selection on a case-by-case basis have never been conducted; guidance for deviating from the accepted standards is lacking at this time.

3.7.1.2 SKEW CONSIDERATIONS.   It was pointed out previously in the case of the conventional single-screw ship wake, Fig. 24, that the shadow of the vessel skeg produces a heavy axial wake defect concentrated along the disk vertical centerline. The blades of conventional propellers ray out from the hub (i.e., the blade midchord lines are more or less straight rays emanating from the hub centerline). Such "unskewed" blades abruptly encounter the axial velocity defect of the conventional stern wake at the top and bottom dead-center blade positions. The radially *in-phase* character of the abrupt encounter results in high net blade loads and radiated pressure.

A more gradual progression of the blades through the vertical wake defect is accomplished by curving the blade midchord lines. Different radii enter and leave the wake spike at different times; cancellation results in the radial integrations to blade loads and radiated pressure, with the result of sometimes drastically reduced vibratory excitation. Two such successfully used *skewed* propellers are shown in Fig. 25, from Hammer and McGinn (1978).

Skew will work less effectively with strut-stern wakes, since the axial velocity defect tends to be concentrated more in the outer extreme radii. The more radially uniform distributions of the conventional stem case with which to achieve as high a degree of *dephasing* and radial cancellation are generally not available with the strut stern. Of course, the strut-stern vessel is in less need of propeller design extremes, as vibration problems are already essentially eliminated by the stern form selection, provided proper clearances are incorporated.

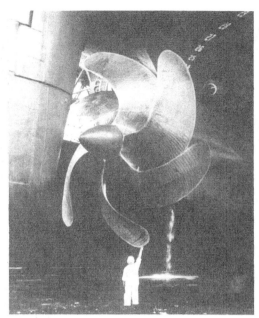

(a) *Sea Bridge* Class

(b) *San Clemente* Class

Fig. 25 Highly skewed propeller installations.

Care must be taken in incorporating skew, particularly in replacement propellers, that adequate clearances between the blade tips and the rudder be maintained. As the blades are skewed in the pitch helix, the tips move downstream, closing up blade tip/rudder clearances.

The consequences can be increased hull vibratory forces transmitted through the rudder, as well as rudder erosion caused by the collapsing sheet cavitation shed downstream off the blade tips as they sweep through the top of the propeller disk. The recourse is to incorporate warp into the blades along with the skew. Warping is a forward raking of the skewed blades back to (and sometimes beyond) the propeller disk. It is equivalent to skewing the blades in the plane of the disk rather than in the pitch helix.

It should be noted for the sake of completeness that skew has a beneficial effect in reducing the effects of vibration-producing fluctuating sheet cavitation, even when such cavitation may be concentrated at the blade tips. The blade curvature is thought to result in a radially outward flow component in the vicinity of the blade tips, which tends to sweep the cavity sheets into the tip vortex, where the critical collapse phase usually occurs more gradually downstream.

3.7.1.3 HARMONIC ANALYSIS. It is necessary to progress beyond mere descriptive considerations of hull wake for ensuring achievement of acceptably small propeller excitation. Harmonic, or Fourier, analysis of the predicted wake is required in almost all procedures for assessing propeller excitation severity.

The axial and tangential wake velocity components (see Fig. 24) can be written as the following Fourier series in position angle θ, for selected radii.

$$\frac{v_x(r,\theta)}{U} \approx \frac{V_a(r)}{U} + \mathrm{Re}\sum_{q=1}^{Q} C_{xq}(r)e^{iq\theta}$$

$$\frac{v_T(r,\theta)}{U} \approx \mathrm{Re}\sum_{q=1}^{Q} C_{T_q}(r)e^{iq\theta} \qquad (142)$$

In equation (142), $V_a(r)/U$ is the steady circumferentially average axial velocity, which is the radially varying speed of advance through the propeller disc; the steady average tangential velocity is taken as zero, since ship wakes have negligible steady *swirl*. The prefix Re denotes the *real part* of the complex series, as previously noted, and $e^{iq\theta}$ is, by identity

$$e^{iq\theta} \equiv \cos q\theta + i \sin q\theta$$

The complex coefficients $C_{xq}(r)$ and $C_{T_q}(r)$ are determined from the numerical wake data using the formula

$$C_q(r) = \frac{1}{\pi}\int_{\theta=-\pi}^{\pi} \frac{v(r,\theta)}{U} e^{-iq\theta} d\theta \qquad (143)$$

The series in equation (142) are truncated at Q terms, and are therefore denoted as approximations. It has been found that a value of Q on the order of 10 reproduces wake contours, typically Fig. 24, with reasonable accuracy. For Q values no higher than approximately 10, it has also been found that the coefficients in equation (142) can be calculated with acceptable accuracy by employing Simpson's rule at equation (143), with points spaced at even 5-degree increments. Using this procedure, the coefficients are calculated as

$$C_q(r) = \frac{1}{108} \sum_{j=1}^{73} W_j \frac{v(r, \theta_j)}{U} e^{-iq\theta_j} \qquad (144)$$

where $\theta_j = -\pi + (j-1)\pi/36$ in radians, and the W_j are the Simpson's multipliers, $W_j = 1, 4, 2, 4, \ldots, 4, 1$.

Given the wake data in the form of Fig. 24, equation (139) is executed for $q = 1$ to 10 for typically eight different radii in the propeller disc; the eight radial stations are usually $r/R = 0.25, 0.35, \ldots, 0.95$.

When executing equations (143) or (144), it will be found that for single-screw ships, the $C_{xq}(r)$ values are pure real, and the $C_{Tq}(r)$ values are pure imaginary. This is due to the symmetry of single-screw ship wakes. For multi-screw ship wakes, both the real and imaginary parts of both sets of coefficients will be nonzero, in general.

3.7.2 Approximate Selection of Propeller Blade Skew. As discussed in the last section, if one is forced to accept the highly irregular wake imposed by the conventional single-screw stern, then propeller blade skew may be an alternative means for limiting the propeller-induced vibratory excitation to acceptable levels.

Skew is normally specified as an angle in the projected plane of the blade. Skew angle is defined in Fig. 26 and denoted $\alpha_s(r)$; it is the angle at some radius r in the projected view between the ray bisecting the blade section at the hub, and the ray bisecting the blade section at r. Percentage skew is given by the formula

$$\% \ skew = \alpha_s(R)N \times 100/360 \qquad (145)$$

where $\alpha_s(R)$ is the skew angle at the blade tip and N is the number of blades. By equation (140), 100% skew, for example, corresponds to the tip of one blade lying on the generator line through the root of the follow-ing blade; both of the propellers shown in Fig. 25 have 100% skew. High skew is considered to be 50% or more. While skew is always made positive, or zero, at the blade tip, it is often negative at intermediate radii; the skew angle is conventionally positive counterclockwise, looking forward.

The increasing use of controllable pitch propellers (CPPs) with diesel and gas turbine engines has led to an alternative definition of blade skew. This is the blade tip angle less the maximum negative angle of the blade leading edge, which occurs at an intermediate radius. This is to reflect the leading edge sweep needed for spindle torque reduction that is employed in CPPs.

Actually, leading edge sweep has been proposed by some as the best definition of skew from the standpoint of force reduction.

The idea of skew, as previously explained, is to synchronize the lift fluctuations over the radii of the blades in such a way that cancellations occur in the radial integrations. By shifting the blade sections unequally along the helices, the sections can be made to enter the regions of wake concentration at different angles, with the result of reduced net forces.

Actually, rough judgments as to effective amounts of blade skew for a given application can be made from the wake data alone, without any explicit calculations of forces at all. This procedure was proposed by Cumming, Morgan, and Boswell (1972), and is as follows.

Referring to Fig. 26, the relative velocity normal to the blade section at (r, θ) is

$$v_n(r, \theta) = -v_x \cos \beta_G + (\Omega r + v_t) \sin \beta_G \qquad (146)$$

where $v_x(r, \theta)$ and $v_t(r, \theta)$ are the axial and tangential nominal wake velocities and $\beta_G(r)$ is the blade geometric pitch angle. Normal velocity is important to the magnitude of the propeller blade pressure distribution; by linear theory, the pressure distribution is, in fact, proportional to the normal velocity distribution, as is shown subsequently.

It is convenient to replace β_G by β in equation (146). The slightly smaller hydrodynamic advance angle eliminates the specific blade particulars, for convenience. From Fig. 26,

$$\tan\beta = \frac{V_a(r)}{\Omega r} = \frac{V_a(r)/U}{(\pi/J)(r/R)} \qquad (147)$$

where J is the advance ratio, U/nD. The difference in β and β_G is not within the accuracy of this exercise.

Substituting the wake Fourier series, equation (142), into equation (146)

$$\frac{v_n(r,\theta)}{U} = -\frac{V_a(r)}{U}\cos\beta + \Omega r \sin\beta$$
$$+ \mathrm{Re} \sum_{q=1}^{Q} V_{nq}(r)e^{iq\theta} \qquad (148)$$

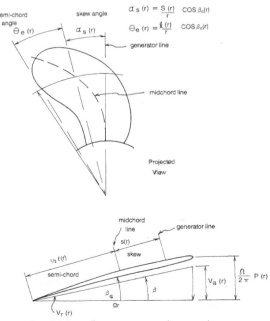

Fig. 26 Propeller geometry and nomenclature.

The qth harmonic normal velocity complex amplitude in equation (148) is

$$V_{nq} = -C_{xq} \cos \beta + C_{T_q} \sin \beta \qquad (149)$$

with $C_{xq}(r)$ and $C_{Tq}(r)$ being the qth harmonic axial and tangential wake Fourier coefficients from equation (144). Equation (148) can be written alternatively as

$$\frac{v_n(r,\theta)}{U} \cong \sum_{q=0}^{Q} \frac{v_{nq}(r,\theta)}{U}$$

where, for harmonic q,

$$\frac{v_{nq}(r)}{U} = |V_{nq}| \cos(q\theta - \gamma_q) \qquad (150)$$

In equation (150),

$$|V_{nq}| = \sqrt{\left(V_{nq}^{R}\right)^2 + \left(V_{nq}^{I}\right)^2}$$

and

$$\gamma_q = \tan^{-1}(-V_{nq}^{I}/V_{nq}^{R}) \qquad (151)$$

with the superscripts R and I denoting real and imaginary parts.

Values of q in equation (150) correspond to maximum values of the wake normal velocity, which occur for

$$\cos(q\theta - \gamma_q) = 1$$

giving

$$q\theta - \gamma_q(r) = 2n\pi; \; n = 0, 1, \ldots$$

The blade position angles for maximum normal velocity at the section r midchord line are therefore

$$\theta(r) = (\gamma_q(r) + 2n\pi)/q; \; n = 0, 1, 2, \ldots \qquad (152)$$

$\theta(r)$ can be plotted versus r from equation (152) to show contour lines of the normal velocity maxima in the propeller disk. A skew-line of $\alpha_s(r)$ versus r can then be sketched that interferes appropriately with the $\theta(r)$ lines to imply the desired cancellation. This procedure is best illustrated with the following example.

Table 3 shows the computation of $\theta(r)$ from equation (152) for the fourth harmonic of the Series 60, $C_B = 0.6$, wake (Stuntz, Pien, Hinterthan, & Ficken, 1960), which is essentially that depicted in Fig. 24. The computations are performed at eight radii, as indicated.

A value of J of 0.834 was used. The same calculation for $q = 3$ was also performed. The $\theta(r)$ versus r curves by equation (152) are plotted for $q = 3$ in Fig. 27 and for $q = 4$ in Fig. 28. The solid lines in the figures are the normal velocity maxima corresponding to $n = -1, 0, 1$ for $q = 3$ and to $n = -1, 0, 1, 2$ for $q = 4$. The dashed lines are the normal velocity minima midway between the maxima.

Assume, for purposes of example, that alternating propeller thrust is of primary concern, and should therefore dictate the skew selection. Also assume that a four-bladed propeller is to be used. As shown in Section 2, for N propeller blades, blade-rate alternating thrust, as well as torque, is produced exclusively by the Nth wake harmonic (i.e., $q = 4$ in this example). Therefore, based on the $q = 4$ curves of Fig. 28, a linearly varying skew of 40 degrees, or 44%, is selected. This is the line

Table 3 Locus of Normal Velocity Maxima for Fourth Harmonic of Series 60, $C_B = 0.6$, wake $J = 0.834$

r/R	0.25	0.35	0.45	0.55	0.65	0.75	0.85	0.95
Va/U	0.522	0.640	0.736	0.791	0.813	0.818	0.828	0.845
β, degrees, equation (147)	0.0	26.2	23.5	20.9	18.4	16.1	14.5	13.3
C_{x4} equation (144)	0.0	0.0475	−0.0747	−0.0802	−0.0705	−0.0567	−0.0460	−0.0370
C_{T4}	0.0201 i	0.0184 i	0.0173 i	0.0137 i	0.0089 i	0.0075 i	0.0056 i	0.0062 i
$V_{n4} = -C_{x4} \cos \beta$ equation (149)	0.0	0.0426	0.0685	0.0749	0.0669	0.05435	0.0445	0.0360
$V_{n4} = +C_{T4} \sin \beta$ equation (149)	0.0097 i	0.0081 i	0.0069 i	0.0049 i	0.0028 i	0.0021 i	0.0056 Ii	0.0014 Ii
γ_4, degrees, equation (151)	−90.0	−10.8	−5.8	−3.7	−2.4	−2.2	−1.8	−2.2
θ, degrees, equation (152) $n = -1$	−112.5	−92.7	−91.5	−90.9	−90.6	−90.6	−90.5	−90.6
$n = 0$	−22.5	−2.7	−1.5	−0.93	−0.60	−0.55	−0.45	−0.55
$n = 1$	67.5	87.3	88.5	89.1	89.4	89.5	89.6	89.5
$n = 2$	157.5	177.3	178.5	179.1	179.4	179.5	179.6	179.5

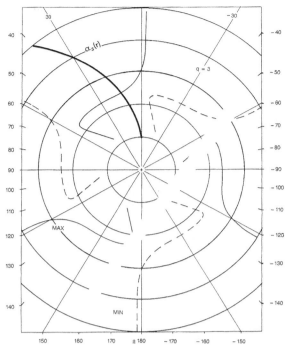

Fig. 27 Nominal wake maxima, Series 60, third harmonic in the circumferentially nonuniform wake.

denoted $\alpha_s(r)$ in Fig. 28. Rotating this line in θ shows that roughly equal parts of the blade fall in regions of positive and negative normal velocity at all times; this skew distribution should therefore produce the desired

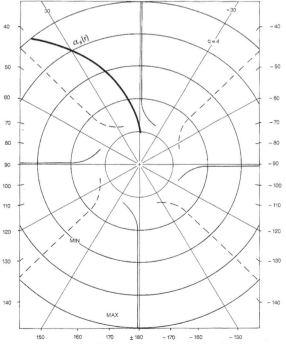

Fig. 28 Nominal wake maxima, Series 60, fourth harmonic.

radial cancellation and result in significantly reduced unsteady thrust over that which would be developed by an unskewed blade.

The linear 44% skew distribution selected is also drawn on the third harmonic wake contour plot in Fig. 27. Here, as the skew line is shifted in θ, it is seen that some degree of radial interference also occurs but not to the same degree as with $q = 4$. The critical midregion of the blade, between approximately the 0.4 and 0.8 radii, still encounters roughly in-phase normal velocity maxima and minima with the 40-degree skew. From the bearing force formula of Section 2, equation (93), the third- and fifth-wake harmonics produce the lateral bearing forces and moments for four blades; the lower harmonic, in this case the third, usually dominates because of the convergence of the wake Fourier series. Therefore, in this example, the propeller designer might also expect some reduction in the lateral bearing forces and moments on incorporating 44% skew, but not as much as in the alternating thrust.

Actually, cases occur in the exercise demonstrated by this example in which, with any possible consecutive sequence of wake harmonics around blade number, some normal velocity contours are skewed (out-of-phase radially) and some are unskewed. Since the general rule is that the blade should be skewed if the wake is unskewed, and vice versa, it may then be impossible in such cases to avoid actually increasing certain bearing force components when decreasing others with skew incorporation. This is often the case with the single-screw conventional stern merchant ship wake; it can be seen to a slight degree in the third and fourth harmonics of the Series 60, $C_B = 0.6$ wake in Figs. 27 and 28. The even wake harmonics are characteristically unskewed and the odd harmonics are characteristically skewed in this wake type (Cumming et al., 1972). An order of importance of the various force components must therefore be established beforehand in such cases to provide a rational basis for the skew selection.

3.7.3 Estimation of Propeller Bearing Forces. As described to some depth in Section 2, the propeller excitation consists of a set of three force and three moment components acting in the propeller hub, plus a distribution of unsteady pressure over the after-hull surfaces.

The propeller hub forces, or bearing forces, are the collective effects at the propeller hub of the unsteady blade pressure resulting from operation of the propeller in the circumferentially nonuniform wake.

The formula for calculating the bearing force components is developed in Section 2, as formula (92). This formula is written in terms of the radial distribution of unsteady blade lift, denoted $Lq(r)$. As discussed in Section 2, $Lq(r)$ can be estimated by various approaches, with various levels of accuracy and needing various levels of effort. One procedure that is relatively simple to apply, and is at least accurate enough for meaningful relative evaluations for variations in design parameters, such as wake and skew, is the two-dimensional *gust theory* of von Karman and Sears (1938), applied strip-wise (Lewis, 1963). It has the following form:

$$Lq(r) = \rho U^2 R C_{Lq}(r) \tag{153}$$

with

$$C_{Lq}(r) = \pi \frac{V_r(r)}{U} \frac{l(r)}{R} V_{nq}(r) \overline{C}_s(r, k^*) e^{iq\alpha_s(r)}$$

The variables in equation (153) are the following.

$Lq(r)$: q^{th} harmonic complex lift amplitude distribution
ρ: fluid density
U: ship speed
R: propeller radius
$V_r(r)$: relative velocity tangent to blade section pitch line. From Fig. 26, ignoring the propeller self-induced velocities,

$$V_r(r) = \sqrt{V_a^2 + \Omega^2 r^2}$$

or

$$\frac{V_r(r)}{U} = \sqrt{\left(\frac{V_a}{U}\right)^2 + \left(\frac{\pi}{J} \frac{r}{R}\right)^2} \tag{154}$$

with $J = U/nD$.

$V_{ng}(r)$ – q^{th} harmonic complex wake velocity normal to blade section pitch line at r. This is essentially equation (149), but definition of the normal using the true geometric pitch rather than the hydrodynamic advance (see Fig. 26) is recommended:

$$V_{nq}(r) = -C_{xq} \cos \beta_G + C_{T_q} \sin \beta_G \tag{155}$$

Here $C_{xq}(r)$ and $C_{T_q}(r)$ are q^{th} harmonic axial and tangential wake coefficients from equation (144) (and Table 3), and β_G is the geometric pitch angle. From Fig. 26,

$$\begin{aligned}\tan \beta_G(r) &= \frac{P(r)}{2\pi r} \\ &= \frac{P(r)/D}{\pi(r/R)}\end{aligned} \tag{156}$$

where $P(r)$ is the blade pitch distribution.

$\ell(r)$ in equation (153) is the blade section chord length at r (in the expanded view) (see Fig. 26). $\overline{C}_s(r, k^*)$ is the complex conjugate of the Sears function, from Fig. 29. This is an Argand diagram that gives the real and imaginary parts of C_s as a function of the section reduced frequency, k^*.

$$C_s = C_s^R + i C_s^I$$

The reduced frequency is defined as

$$k^*(r) = q\theta_e(r) \tag{157}$$

where q is the harmonic order, and θ_e is the blade section projected semichord angle. In terms of the section chord length $l(r)$,

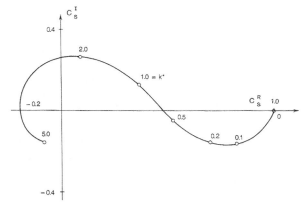

Fig. 29 Sears function $C_s(k^*)$.

$$\theta_e(r) = \frac{1}{2}\left[\frac{l/R \cos\beta_G}{r/R}\right] \tag{158}$$

where $\alpha_s(r)$ is the blade section skew angle, in radians (see Fig. 26). The f_{ip} of equations (91) and (92) can be manipulated into the following form useful for computation.

$$f_{ip}(\theta) = \sum_{m=1}^{\infty} |F_{ipm}| \cos mN(\theta - \beta_{ipm}) \tag{159}$$

where the blade position angle $\theta = -\Omega t$ from Fig. 8. N is blade number in equation (159) so that the series represents the superposition of blade-rate harmonics. F_{ipm} is the mth blade-rate harmonic complex amplitude of the ith force component. The real amplitude and phase angle in equation (159) are given in terms of the real and imaginary parts of F_{ipm} as

$$|F_{ipm}| = \sqrt{\left(F_{ipm}^R\right)^2 + \left(F_{ipm}^I\right)^2} \tag{160}$$

and

$$\beta_{ipm} = \frac{1}{mN} \tan^{-1}\left(\frac{-F_{ipm}^I}{F_{ipm}^R}\right) \tag{161}$$

The β_{ipm} in equation (161) corresponds to the position angle of the propeller blade nearest top dead-center when the mth blade-rate harmonic of the ith force component is positive maximum. The positive force directions are indicated on Fig. 8 and the propeller blade position angle, θ, is positive counterclockwise, looking forward.

The fundamental blade-rate harmonic of the bearing forces is usually predominant, so that attention can be restricted to $m = 1$ in equations (159) through (161) in most cases.

If one of the bearing force components must be singled out as most worthy of the designer's attention, it would be the alternating thrust, as the exciter of longitudinal vibration of main propulsion machinery. The hull surface excitation component, rather than the bearing forces, is the more critical direct exciter of the hull, as will be considered later.

Focusing attention on the alternating thrust ($i = 1$) specifically, the complex amplitude from equations (91) and (92) can be written as

$$F_{ipm} = -N \int_{r=rh}^{R} L_{mN}(r)\cos\beta_G(r)\,dr \qquad (162)$$

Here, r_h denotes propeller hub radius, and the lift harmonic order q in equation (153) is mN. In terms of the nondimensional lift coefficient of equation (153), equation (162) can be rewritten as

$$C_{1pm} \equiv \frac{F_{1pm}}{\rho U^2 R^2}$$
$$= -N \int_{r=rh/R}^{1.0} C_{LmN}(r)\cos\beta_G(r)\,dr \qquad (163)$$

For purposes of computation, a rectangle rule integration at eight equally spaced radial stations is of commensurate accuracy with that of the recommended formulas. For $r_h/R = 0.2$, which is the usual case, equation (163) becomes

$$C_{1pm} = -N/10 \sum_{j=1}^{8} C_{LmN_j}\cos\beta_{G_j} \qquad (164)$$

The steps in the computation by equation (164) are illustrated in the following example.

Consider an NSMB Series B.4 propeller (Troost, 1937–1951) with four blades, operating in the Series 60, $C_B = 0.6$ wake of the previous example. A propeller which matches the Series 60 wake and the J of 0.834 has a $P(r)/D = 1.024$ at $r/R = 0.7$ and an expanded area ratio of 0.471. Table 4 outlines the computation of the blade-rate alternating thrust coefficient, C_{1p1}, from equation (163).

First of all, the phase angle, β_{1p1}, from Table 4 is sensible. $\beta_{1p1} = 42.4$ degrees implies that the alternating thrust is maximum aft (positive) when a propeller blade is 42.4 degrees before top dead-center (with right-hand rotation clockwise looking forward). But the blade-rate alternating thrust executes four complete cycles, each of 90 degrees duration, in one 360-degree revolution. The thrust therefore alternates in direction from maximum aft to maximum forward in 45 degrees. The phase angle of 42.4 degrees therefore corresponds to a blade position of –2.6 degrees, or effectively at top dead-center, when the alternating thrust is maximum forward. This is intuitively satisfactory.

Table 4   Blade-Rate Alternating Thrust Coefficient, NSMB B.4 Prop, P/D = 1.02, Ear = 0.471 Series 60, C_B = 0.6

r/R	0.25	0.35	0.45	0.55	0.65	0.75	0.85	0.95
P/D	0.876	0.945	0.999	1.024	1.024	1.024	1.024	1.024
l/R	0.418	0.465	0.500	0.518	0.521	0.497	0.428	0.305
α_s, rad	0.023	0.060	0.105	0.143	0.160	0.190	0.232	0.275
β_G, deg, (156)	48.12	40.68	35.25	30.65	26.64	23.49	20.98	18.94
θ_e, rad, (158)	0.558	0.504	0.454	0.405	0.358	0.304	0.235	0.152
k', (157)	2.23	2.02	1.82	1.62	1.43	1.22	0.94	0.61
$\frac{V_a}{U}$, Table 2	0.522	0.640	0.736	0.791	0.813	0.818	0.828	0.845
$\frac{V_p}{U}$ (154)	1.077	1.465	1.848	2.218	2.580	2.941	3.307	3.677
$C_8 = C_8^R + iC_8^I$ (Fig. 29)	0.018	0.077	0.133	0.190	0.245	0.307	0.385	0.485
	0.226i	0.269i	0.262i	0.245i	0.220i	0.177i	0.109i	−002i
C_{x4} Table 2	0.	−.0475	−.0747	−.0802	−.0705	−.0567	−.0460	−.0370
C_{T4}	0.0201i	0.0184i	0.0173i	0.0137i	0.0089i	0.0075i	0.0056i	0.0062i
$V_{nq} = -C_{x4}\cos\beta_G + C_{T4}$	0.	0.0360	0.0610	0.0690	0.0630	0.0520	0.0430	0.0350
$\sin\beta_G$ (155)	0.0150i	0.0120i	0.0100i	0.0070i	0.0040i	0.0030i	0.0020i	0.0020i
$C_{L4} = (C_{L4}^R + iC_{L4}^I) \times$	.4750	1.694	4.579	7.740	8.777	8.112	5.858	2.384
10^{-2} (153)	.0823i	−1.518i	−2.165i	−1.831i	.2500t	2.560i	4.921i	5.494i
$C_{1p1} = (C_{1p1}^R + i\,C_{1p1}^I) \times$								−13.93
10^{-2} (163)								−2.810
$|C_{1p1}|$, (160)								0.142
β_{1p1}, deg, (161)								42.2

The force coefficient of $|C_{1p1}| = 0.152$ from Table 4 is a typical value for cases for which specific measures have not been taken to reduce vibratory excitation. Alternating thrust amplitude is often expressed as a percentage of steady thrust. Assume that the propeller and wake of Table 3 belong to a ship with 17,800 DHP and a speed of 20 knots. Assume that the propeller diameter is 6 m. Then,

$$|F_{1p1}| = 0.142\rho\ U^2 R^2 = 14.2\ t$$

Taking a QPC of 0.65 and a thrust deduction fraction of 0.1 as typical values, the steady thrust for this vessel would be

$$T = \frac{550 DHP \cdot QPC}{U(1-t)} = 134\ t$$

The alternating thrust in this example is therefore 10.6% of the steady thrust.

Now, the skew of the NSMB series propeller blade is relatively low; it is 16.7% at the blade tip, as can be deduced from Table 4. It was judged in the example of the preceding section that a significant reduction in alternating over that of an unskewed propeller operating in the Series 60 wake could be achieved with a linearly varying skew out to 40 degrees at the tip, or 44% with the four-bladed propeller.

The Table 4 computation has been repeated in Table 5 with the above increased skew, and with all other propeller geometric data held fixed (a slight pitch adjustment would actually have to accompany the new skew distribution to maintain the same performance, but this is higher order to the unsteady force computations). A drop in $|C_{1p1}|$ from 0.142 to 0.106 on increasing skew from 16.7% to 44% represents a 25% reduction in alternating thrust. Greater increases in skew would result in greater reductions in alternating thrust. In fact, skew distributions can theoretically be found which result in zero alternating thrust. The 100% skew distributions that have been incorporated with the conventional single screw merchant ship wake on several occasions (see Fig. 25) typically approach this limit. However, as was described relative to the example of the preceding

section, skew distributions designed to accomplish reductions in a single bearing force component, such as alternating thrust, will generally not reduce the other force components by the same degree, and some increases may even occur.

To demonstrate this last point, the vertical bearing force corresponding to the propeller and wake of Table 4 was calculated. Formula (92) for $i = 3$ was implemented in a similar tabular format as Table 5. As indicated by formula (92), the blade-rate lateral forces and moments are due to the wake harmonics to either side of blade number, versus the blade number harmonic in the case of alternating thrust. It is convenient to write the respective complex amplitudes for $i = 2, 3, 5,$ and 6 (see Fig. 8) in the following form.

$$F_{ipm} = F_{ipm}^{\ +} + F_{ipm}^{\ -}$$
$$= \rho U^2 R^2 \left(C_{ipm}^{\ +} + C_{ipm}^{\ -} \right) \quad (165)$$

Here the + and − superscripts denote the contributions of the $mN + 1$ and $mN - 1$ wake harmonics, respectively. For blade-rate ($m = 1$) excitation with the four-bladed example propeller, the lift harmonics corresponding to $q = 3$ and $q = 5$ were evaluated by equation (129) and substituted into the respective $i = 3$ formula of equation (92). For the original NSMB propeller of Table 3, this computation produced the following vertical force components.

$$C_{3p1}^{\ +} = (0.5020 + 0.3740i)10^{-2}\ C_{3p1}^{\ -} = (-1.650 + 1.248i)10^{-2} \quad (166)$$

From equation (166),

$$|C_{3p1}| = 0.0199$$

This coefficient corresponds to 1.49% of the 134-ton steady thrust of the example ship and is a typical value for the conventional stern merchant ship wake. For the propeller with greater skew (see Table 5), on the other hand,

$$C_{3p1}^{\ +} = (.1260 + 0.72920i)10^{-2}$$
$$C_{3p1}^{\ -} = (-1.886 - 1.590i)10^{-2}$$

Table 5 Blade-Rate Alternating Thrust Coefficient, Repeat of Table 4 Computation with Increased Blade Skew*

r/R	0.25	0.35	0.45	0.55	0.65	0.75	0.85	0.95
α_s, rad	0.0436	0.1309	0.2182	0.3054	0.3927	0.4800	0.5672	0.6545
$C_{L4} = (C_{L4}^{\ R} + iC_{L4}^{\ I}) \times 10^{-2}$	0.4667	2.051	5.261	7.112	5.442	0.9842	-3.456	-5.362
	0.1211i	−0.9832i	−0.3480i	3.102i	6.891i	8.419i	6.825i	2.670i
$C_{1p1} = (C_{1p1}^{\ R} + iC_{1p1}^{\ I}) \times 10^{-2}$								−3.900
								−9.800i
$|C_{1p1}|$								0.1055
β_{1p1}, deg								27.9

*Only data that are different from Table 4 are included in Table 5.

Again, from equation (166)

$$|C_{3p1}| = 0.0193$$

The comparison predicts that the vertical bearing force decreases by 3% with the skew increase. The probability of a lateral force reduction less than achieved in alternating thrust (26%) was to be expected on the basis of Figs. 27 and 28, as described in the associated example.

While the relatively simple two-dimensional approximation of lift by equation (148) is considered to be reliable for the types of relative evaluations represented by the preceding examples, a warning is in order with regard to the interpretation and use of the absolute magnitudes so predicted. Applying the two-dimensional theory stripwise, as is suggested, is equivalent to assuming that the propeller blade has infinite aspect ratio (span to chord ratio) in regard to the evaluation of the self-induced velocities, which is accomplished by the Sears function in equation (153). This assumption results in a not insignificant overestimate of lift for aspect ratios typical of marine propeller blades. The approximate degree of overestimate can be judged with the aid of Fig. 30 (Breslin, 1970). This figure applies to rectangular wings, of aspect ratios 1 and 4, traversing sinusoidal gusts of reduced frequency k^*. The ordinate is the ratio of unsteady lift calculated by the two-dimensional strip-wise approximation, equation (129), to that calculated by a lifting surface theory which allows for the finite aspect ratio effects. On consideration that the aspect ratios of marine propellers are typically on the order of 2 to 3 and reduced frequencies are on the order of 1 to 2, Fig. 30 suggests lift overestimates on the order of 30% to 50% by the two-dimensional formulation. This is consistent with the conclusion of the comparative analysis of various propeller force calculation procedures reported in Boswell, Kim, Jessup, and Lin (1983). However, the proposed two-dimensional formulation incorporates all of the design variables, other than aspect ratio, in the cor-

rect physical structure, and is therefore, as previously stated, useful in the design type of trade-off investigations where the premium is on reliable relative evaluations. It is consistent with the proposed objective of minimizing the propeller excitation within the normal design constraints, which requires force evaluations with reasonably high relative, rather than absolute, accuracy.

An alternative simple method for calculating propeller vibratory bearing forces is that of Tanibayashi (1980). This method is essentially the quasisteady method of McCarthy (1961), with semiempirical modifications to allow for nonzero frequency effects. The comparisons of the latter reference suggest that the Tanibayashi method may have better absolute accuracy than the two-dimensional unsteady strip method for some ranges of the variables. However, the Tanibayashi method, being less rational, does not appear to be as generally reliable in predicting the correct trends with changes in the variables. As discussed above, this characteristic is important to the relative accuracy required in many design considerations. For the types of design exercises illustrated by the preceding examples (as well as those to follow), the two-dimensional unsteady strip method is recommended over other methods of the simple type.

3.7.4 Estimation of Propeller-Induced Hull Surface Excitation.

Other than in the case of longitudinal vibration of main propulsion machinery and some main shafting vibration problems, the propeller bearing forces covered in the immediately preceding section are of secondary importance; the hull surface force excitation is the primary source in propeller-induced ship vibration. But this is only because of the common occurrence of some degree of moderate fluctuating sheet cavitation on the propeller blades. As discussed to some depth in Section 2, the bearing forces are relatively insensitive to fluctuating sheet cavitation, and it is usually ignored in their analysis. This is not the case, however, with the hull surface excitation; fluctuating sheet cavitation can amplify the propeller-induced hull surface pressures and resultant forces by easily an order of magnitude over the noncavitating levels. The occurrence of propeller cavitation cannot be ignored in attempts to quantify propeller-induced hull surface excitation and resultant hull vibration.

Unfortunately, while developing rapidly, the state-of-the-art has not yet produced a methodology for design stage estimation of hull surface excitation of relative accuracy and utility equal to that available for bearing force estimation. Wilson (1981) summarized the simple formulas and criteria then available to the designer for dealing with hull surface excitation. Wilson compared the various proposed formulations against data from the few cases of recent U.S. Naval ship vibration problems and concluded that none of the formulations appeared capable of providing reliable indications about the likelihood of ship vibration trouble. Theoretical irra-

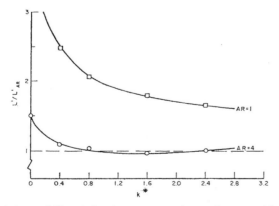

Fig. 30 Ratio of lift calculated using unsteady two-dimensional formula stripwise to exact unsteady result for aspect ratios 1 and 4.

tionality is no doubt responsible, in large part, for the inadequacy of the quick estimation techniques then, and currently, available; they are, for the most part, little more than rules of thumb based simply on intuition and empiricism.

Actually, experience has shown that if wake nonuniformity is at least not ignored in stern-lines design, and if state-of-the-art propeller design is employed, which includes incorporating blade skew for bearing force control and maintenance of cavitation inception standards (Cox & Morgan, 1972), then serious vibration will seldom occur. Nevertheless, a simple, rational, though incomplete, formulation for hull surface force prediction is outlined in the remainder of this section. While the formulation should be of some limited utility to the designer in its present form, it is presented mainly as a rational framework to be filled out as the state-of-the-art in this area advances.

As vertical hull vibration has been identified as the main girder vibration of concern, attention is focused here on the vertical component of the hull surface force. Hull surface force, rather than pressure, is considered to be the more appropriate measure of merit of hull surface excitation for minimization considerations, on the basis of the reasons cited in Section 2. The noncavitating and cavitating cases are considered separately.

3.7.4.1 NONCAVITATING VERTICAL HULL SURFACE FORCES. Vorus, Breslin, and Tein (1978) derive the following formula, based on reciprocity (Section 2) for the complex amplitude of a noncavitating hull vertical surface force coefficient.

$$C_{3hm}^{NC} = -C_{1pm} v_{30x}^*$$
$$-iC_{3PM}^- v_{31\theta}^* + iC_{3pm}^+ \bar{v}_{31\theta}^* \qquad (167)$$

The terms in equation (162) are the following.

C_{3hm}^{NC}: m^{th} blade-rate harmonic vertical ($i = 3$) noncavitating hull surface force coefficient;

$$F_{3hm}^{NC} = \rho U^2 R^2 C_{3hm}^{NC}$$

C_{1pm}: m^{th} blade-rate harmonic alternating thrust coefficient (e.g., Tables 4 and 5)

C_{3Pm}^+: m^{th} blade-rate harmonic vertical bearing force coefficients corresponding $mN + 1$ (+) and $mN - 1$ (−) wake harmonic contributions (e.g., equation [164])

v_{30x}^* and $v_{31\theta}^*$: velocities induced in the propeller disk by vertically downward unit velocity motion of the bare hull, as described in Vorus, Breslin, and Tein (1978). $\bar{v}_{31\theta}^*$ is the complex conjugate of $v_{31\theta}^*$.

Formula (167) applies to the stern type for which the breadth of the counter directly above the propeller can be characterized as large. It is unfortunately not applicable to the case of the cruiser type stern of conventional single screw merchant ships, whose counter is narrow. For the broad stern type, however, for which the propeller bearing forces have been estimated, formula

(167) can be used to estimate the noncavitating vertical hull surface force provided that the bare–hull-induced velocity data is available.

Table 6 gives approximate average values of the required induced velocity data appropriate for use with single-screw and twin-screw ships.

The numbers in the table are approximate averages from detailed calculations of the induced velocities for many ship cases. The tangential velocity component, $v_{31\theta}^*$, is most sensitive to waterplane breadth over the propeller; $v_{31\theta}^*$ increases with waterplane breadth. The extreme value of $v_{31\theta}^*$ that has been encountered, approximately $-0.6i$, was for a single-screw, barge-stern laker where the ratio of waterplane breadth aft to propeller diameter approached 4.0. The more sensitive of the velocity components to stern geometry is, however, the axial component, v_{30x}, in equation (167). This component depends most strongly on the axial distance from the propeller to the waterplane ending. For propeller inset distance denoted x, the extreme values of v_{30x}^* encountered have been 0.15 for a twin-screw naval cruiser with deep inset $D/x_0 \sim 0.5$, and 0.75 for the same barge-stern single-screw laker with a very shallow inset $D/x_0 \sim 2$. A few of the cases for which this data has been evaluated are described by Vorus, Breslin, and Tein (1978).

In the following example, assume a broad countered single-screw ship with a skeg, configured such that the Series 60 wake of Fig. 24 is reasonably representative (this is assumed for example only; a wake evaluated from model tests should be used in actual analysis). Also assume that the propeller is the NSMB B.4 subject of the examples in the preceding section. The bearing force coefficients required in equation (167) for blade-rate surface force evaluation are therefore the values from Table 4 and equation (166). That is

$$C_{1p1} = (-1.50 - 0.272i)10^{-2}$$
$$C_{3p1}^+ = (0.502 + 0.374i)10^{-2}$$
$$C_{3p1}^- = (-1.65 + 1.25i)10^{-2}$$

Using the induced velocity values corresponding to the single-screw ship case of Table 6, equation (167) gives

$$C_{3h1}^{NC} = 0.0132 - 0.00676 \qquad (168)$$

whose amplitude and phase are

$$|C_{3h1}^{NC}| = 0.0149$$

$$\beta_{3h1}^{NC} = \frac{1}{4}\tan^{-1}\frac{0.00676}{0.0132} = 6.8\,\text{deg}$$

Table 6 Hull-Induced Velocity Data for Use

| | Equation (161) | |
| | (Broad Countered Stern Forms) | |
	v_{31x}^*	$v_{31\theta}^*$
Single screw	0.5	−0.5i
Twin screw	0.3	−0.4 to −0.45i

The noncavitating vertical surface force calculated above is slightly smaller than the vertical bearing force, whose magnitude was calculated in equation (166) as $|C_{3p1}| = 0.0199$.

The most appropriate measure of hull girder vertical vibratory excitation should actually be the net vertical force, represented by the vector addition of the vertical bearing and vertical surface forces. Denoting the net vertical force coefficient as C_{3h1}^{NC},

$$C_{3N1}^{NC} = C_{3h1}^{NC} + C_{3p1}$$

Substituting from equations (166) and (168), for the subject example

$$C_{3N1}^{NC} = (0.174 + 0.9i)10^{-2}$$

with amplitude and phase

$$|C_{3N1}^{NC}| = 0.00956$$

$$\beta_{3N1}^{NC} = -19.9 \text{ deg}$$

Thus, the net vertical force predicted in this example is smaller than both the individual vertical bearing force and vertical surface force components. This is to be expected in the case of the broad countered stern to which equation (167) applies (refer to the discussion of the Breslin condition in Section 2.3). The comparison is shown on the bar graph (Fig. 31); the bar heights denote the percentages of thrust of the example propeller and the numbers at the tops of the bars are the phase angles.

3.7.4.2 CAVITATING VERTICAL HULL SURFACE FORCES. On the basis of reciprocity, as covered in Section 2, Vorus,

Breslin, and Tein (1978) also derive a rational formula for the vertical hull surface force coefficient due to unsteady sheet cavitation. It is

$$C_{3hm}^{c} = imN^2\left(\frac{\pi}{J}\right)\left(\frac{b_0}{R}\right)\left(\frac{\phi_{30}^{*}}{b_0}\right)\left(\frac{\dot{\forall}_{mN}}{UR^2}\right) \quad (169)$$

where

N = propeller blade number
J = advance ratio, U/nD
b_0 = design waterline offset in the vertical plane of the propeller disk
ϕ_{30}^{*} = velocity potential induced in the propeller disk by vertically upward unit velocity motion of the bare hull, as described in Vorus, Breslin, and Tein (1978)
$\dot{\forall}_{mN}$ = the mth harmonic of the cavitation volume velocity variation on one propeller blade

Formula (169), like the noncavitating counterpart (167), is reduced from a general reciprocity formulation on the basis of broad waterplane aft. However, due to more rapid convergence characteristics of the hull induced potential, ϕ_{30}^*, in formula (169) versus the hull-induced velocity components in formula (167), formula (169) has been found to work quite well for vessels whose sterns are characterized as narrow. Furthermore, the function ϕ_{30}^*/b_0 has been found to vary only moderately from one stern to the next. In the many detailed calculations of ϕ_{30}^* that have been performed, the extreme values of ϕ_{30}^*/b_0 encountered have been approximately 0.4 and 0.7. However, most fall very close to the average of these extremes; a value of $\phi_{30}^*/b_0 = 0.5$ for all cases should be consistent with the best accuracy achievable in estimating the cavity volume term in formula (169) and with the intended use of the formula.

The illusive term in formula (166) is the cavity volume velocity harmonic, $\dot{\forall}_{mN}$. It is for lack of data in this regard that the cavitating force formula (169) must be held in reserve at this time. However, work has been conducted in pursuing this goal (Lee, 1979; Stern & Vorus, 1983), and is currently being conducted, so that it can be expected that the dynamics of unsteady sheet cavitation will be quantified to the degree needed for, at least, reliable relative evaluations at some point in the future.

Some limited cavitation volume velocity data are, however, available at this time. For example, cavity volume dynamics were estimated by the numerical method of Stern and Vorus (1983) in the excitation force analysis of the Navy oiler documented in Vorus and Associates (1981). The data in this reference are of unsubstantiated accuracy, but it is, at any rate, useful here for demonstrating the character of the required term and the cavitating hull surface force computation by equation (169). This is done in the context of an example.

Figure 32 shows a cavity volume velocity curve calculated by the theory of Stern and Vorus (1983) for the seven-bladed highly skewed propeller of a naval oiler. The x-values on the figure indicate the result of sum-

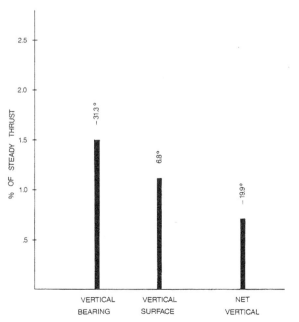

Fig. 31 Blade-rate vertical forces, Series 60, $C_B = 0.60$, NSMB B-Series Propeller.

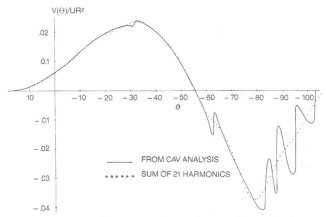

Fig. 32 Estimated cavitation volume velocity, U.S. Naval Oiler.

Table 7 Harmonic Coefficients of Cavitation Volume Velocity for a Naval Oiler

Harmonic Order	q	$\dot{\forall}_q/UR^2 \times 10^{-2}$
0	0.00713	$+i$
1	0.355	$-0.288i$
2	0.733	$+0.196i$
3	0.285	$+0.774i$
4	−0.416	$+0.541i$
5	−0.433	$0.0908i$
6	0.00608	$-0.238i$
7	0.149	$0.0256i$
8	−0.0228	$-0.116i$
9	−0.0795	$0.0139i$
10	0.0185	$0.0573i$
11	0.0539	$+0.0125i$
12	0.0070	$+0.0455i$
13	−0.0287	$+0.0227i$
14	−0.0323	$-0.0127i$
15	−0.00333	$0.0385i$
16	0.0376	$0.0175i$
17	0.0239	$+0.0333i$
18	−0.0326	$+0.0271i$
19	−0.0333	$0.0313i$
20	0.0241	$0.0388i$
21	0.0384	$0.0141i$

ming the Fourier series expansion of the curve using 21 terms; the series is of the form

$$\dot{\forall}(\theta) \cong \mathrm{Re} \sum_{q=0}^{21} \dot{\forall}_q e^{iq\theta} \qquad (170)$$

with the $\dot{\forall}_q$ harmonics calculated using the same general formula as used in the wake harmonic analysis (i.e., equation [144]).

While Fig. 32, as stated, is not of verified accuracy, it cannot be in large error. The expansion commences 10 degrees prior to the blade reaching top dead-center, reaches a maximum volume at around 55 degrees, and terminates in an oscillatory collapse at just over 100 degrees. The mean maximum cavity thickness is estimated from the calculated data to be around 8 cm. All of this is at least consistent with the wake survey and observations from the cavitation tests of the model propeller during the correction phase.

The 21 nondimensional complex $\dot{\forall}_q$ coefficients computed for equation (170) are tabulated in Table 7. In this regard, comparing the calculated and Fourier-fit curves on Table 7, there is clearly significant high harmonic content not covered by the first 21 harmonics.

The oiler is single-screw with a conventional merchant ship stern; $b_0/R = 0.587$ in equation (169). Other relevant data are

$J = 1.032$
$N = 7$
$D = 6.4$ m
$U = 21.4$ knots
thrust, $T = 139$ t

Taking $\phi_{30}^*/b_0 = 0.5$ in equation (169) (the actual calculated value was 0.63), the vertical force coefficient for blade-rate harmonic m is

$$C_{3hm}^c = 55\, im\left(\dot{\forall}_{m7}/UR^2\right) \qquad (171)$$

This coefficient, along with the corresponding fractions of steady thrust, are listed in Table 8 for the first three blade-rate harmonics.

The 7.8% vertical blade-rate force calculated above is not unusually large, as cavitation-induced forces go. Values on the order of 30% of steady thrust are not unheard of. It is, however, seven times larger than the noncavitating surface force from the example of the preceding section (Fig. 33). The naval oiler of this example did, in fact, not have a particularly severe vibration at blade-rate frequency.

The perhaps more alarming aspect of the Table 8 data are the high multiple blade-rate force components. This substantial high harmonic content is a characteristic of the excitation induced by cavitating propellers. It is due, mathematically, to the slow convergence of the volume velocity Fourier series, as is obvious from Table 7. Physically, it is due to the rapid expansion and collapse of the cavitation (see Fig. 32). The strong higher blade-order excitation harmonics of cavitating propellers are quite capable of producing excessive vibration, and also, because of the higher frequencies, excessive noise. The subject naval oiler did, in fact, suffer more from an excessive noise problem, which was attributed to propeller cavitation.

3.8 Propeller Cavitation Noise. Section 2.4 derives formula for calculating far-field radiated noise from a

Table 8 Cavitation I-Induced Vertical Surface Forces

	Blade-Rate $\forall_{m7}/UR^2(10^{-2})$	$\mid C^c_{3hm} \mid \beta_{3hm} \mid F^c_{3hm} \mid$		
	Harmonic m	Equation (170)	Degrees	T
1	$0.149 + 0.0256i$	0.0832	11.5	0.0776
2	$-0.0323 - 0.0127i$	0.0382	-8.0	0.0356
3	$0.0384 - 0.0141i$	0.067	5.3	0.0675

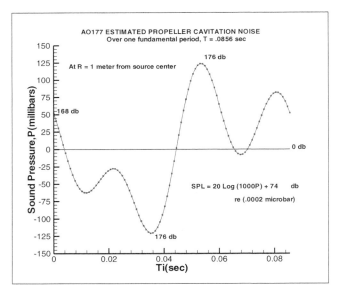

Fig. 33 Oiler P(r, t) and SPL at r = 1 m.

Table 9 Source Acoustic Power Harmonics and Sum

n	λ_n (m)	$\dot{\forall}_n$ (m³/sec)	W_n (watts)
1	120.1	$0.1680-0.0289i$	217.0
2	60.1	$-0.0364-0.0143i$	46.9
3	40.0	$0.0433-0.0159i$	146.9
		$W = \sum W_n = 410.8$	

The operating data listed just above Table 7 gives Ω = 10.48 rad/sec and N = 7 blades. From Section 2, the wave number $k_n = 2\pi/\lambda_n$ with λ_n being the nth harmonic sound wavelength, $\lambda_n = 2\pi c/nN\Omega$. c is the velocity of sound in water, whose nominal value is c = 1403 m/sec (in distilled water at 0 degrees.

Table 9 gives the calculated wave lengths, wave numbers, and power for each of the three blade-order harmonics, and the power sum, by equation (117).

Note that the source sound power is independent of the radius from the source. This is because wave damping has not been included in the derivation via the acoustic wave equation (98).

Note also from Table 9 the lack of convergence of the acoustic power series to three terms. This is again reflected in the same character of the cavitation volume velocity harmonics, implying that the Table 9 calculation is an underestimate of the source power. The maximum frequency of cavitation oscillation represented by Table 7 is 35 Hz in the 21st harmonic. This is a very low frequency in the acoustic range. The threshold frequency for hearing is 20 to 30 Hz. Most presentations of the variation of acoustic data with frequency start at 100 Hz as the lower limit. So again, there is much more frequency content in the Fig. 32 volume velocity curve than was extracted in Table 7, at least for acoustic analysis purposes.

The source power is converted to PWL in dB in Table 10. This is according to equation (119) in Section 2.

The power levels corresponding to the individual harmonics cannot be simply added in dB to obtain the sum, since adding logarithms is not equivalent to adding their arguments. By equation (119),

$$PWL = 10 \log_{10}(W) + 130 = 156 \text{ dB}$$

with W = 410.8 watts from Table 8.

3.8.2 Sound Pressure. PWL is not the most commonly selected acoustic quantity from which to establish criteria for judgment of underwater noise severity. Sound pressure at a point in the far-field is readily measured in noise surveys and experimental programs using

cavitating propeller. Those formulas—equations (108), (116), and (117)—require the same general cavitation volume velocity spectrum, such as is given in Fig. 32 and Table 7 of Section 3.7 for the Navy auxiliary oiler. That example will therefore be continued to underwater radiated underwater noise estimates for the auxiliary oiler for the purpose of demonstrating the basic calculations that are performed.

It must first of all be acknowledged that the Chapter 2 theoretical formulas are quite idealized. They assume far-field transmission through infinite homogeneous liquid with no reflections from the bottom, from the water free surface, or from any body surfaces, and without sound wave energy dissipation. But the model of an oscillating cavity source has been used over the years to model far-field noise (Beranek, 1960; Kinsler & Frey, 1962), and judgments as to noise severity can be made on the basis of these predictions.

3.8.1 Source Power. Formula (117), Section 2.4 expresses the power of the noise source, W. For the three blade-rate harmonics of the cavity volume variation available from Table 7, the power, truncated to three terms, is

$$W = \frac{\rho N^3 \Omega}{8\pi} \sum_{n=1}^{\infty} n k_n \dot{\forall}_{nN} \overline{\dot{\forall}}_{nN} \qquad (117)$$

Table 10 Source Acoustic Power Level, Harmonics, and Sum

n	$PWL_n = 10 \log_{10}(W_n) + 130$ dB
1	153
2	147
3	152

hydrophones. However, sound pressure level (SPL) is a function of radius in the far-field of the source, whereas PWL is not, ideally. From Section 2, formula (108),

$$p(r,t) = \frac{\rho N^2 \Omega}{4\pi r} \operatorname{Re} \sum_{n=1}^{\infty} i n \dot{\forall}_{nN} e^{i(nN\Omega t - \frac{2\pi r}{\lambda_n})} \qquad (108)$$

Because of the dependence on radius, a standard for evaluating sound pressure is at a radius of effectively 1 m from the center of the sound source.

Figure 31 is a plot of the cavitation sound pressure from equation (108) for the oiler over one cycle, $T = 0.0856$ sec, at $r = 1$ m. This radius is certainly not in the far-field of the cavitation source, which is assumed in the derivation of equation (108), but it is used nevertheless as a standard reference radius.

Chapter 15 of Kinsler and Frey (1962) report the SPL of a submerged submarine of 124 dB at 100Hz and at an effective radius $r = 1$ m. The equivalent for a destroyer is claimed to be 10 dB higher than the submarine, and that for an aircraft carrier to be 25 dB higher. On this basis, the prediction of 176 dB in Fig. 31 would project the oiler as a very noisy ship, as-built, and it was.

Of course, the combatant vessels cited by Kinsler and Frey were of early 1960s vintage, and a great deal has

been accomplished in quieting of the U.S. Navy combatant fleet since that time. It is suspected that the far-field noise of modern submarines is hardly above the level of the ambient background of the sea.

A far-field noise prediction using the oiler data in equation (108) is shown in Fig. 34, a plot of sound pressure from 20 to 1000 m from the source, at the time of 0.0668 seconds when the sound pressure was highest at 20 m (which was arbitrary).

A three-dimensional plot of sound pressure versus both r and t would be desirable, but the time and wave length scales differ drastically ($T = 0.0865$ sec compared to $\lambda = 120$ m). The rescaling required in the plotting would limit the perception of the process characteristics desired from a three-dimensional plot.

Ambient sea noise under moderate wind conditions is indicated in Chapter 15 of Kinsler and Frey (1962) to be 50 to 55 dB at 100 Hz. The level of 116 dB at 1000 m from Fig. 31 would be easily detectable at this range, as well as at far greater range, by passive listening devices. In fact, the simple formula (108) predicts that three blade-order harmonics of the estimated Navy oiler propeller blade cavitation would require a distance of 1×10^6 m to fall below the level of the ambient sea noise. This is 540 nautical miles!

The predictive capability of such as formula (108) would be severely degraded at a 500 Nm range due to the compounding effects of all the approximations involved in application of the simple formula to deep-ocean acoustics.

3.8.3 Other. Underwater acoustics, as applied to ships, and to propeller cavitation in particular, has a long history and is well developed, although much the modern technology and understanding has been advanced in military applications and lies in the classified domain.

In the recent open literature, de Jong and de Regt (1998) reviewed the different approaches for the prediction of propeller cavitation noise, namely deterministic, semiempirical, and statistical methods for tonal and broad band noise description. Gesret (2000) presents a comparison of full-scale measurements and a statistical approach for propeller cavitation noise. Bobrovnitskii (2001) has proposed an improved source model for extension into bounded spaces. Research product of this type may not be entirely new, but it is at least openly available to the field of marine dynamics.

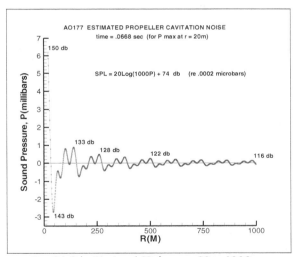

Fig. 34 Oiler P(r, t) and SPL from r = 20 to 1000 m.

4
Criteria, Measurements, and Posttrial Corrections

4.1 Criteria of Acceptable Vibration. It has become more the rule than the exception that new ship specifications require measurement of vibration on builders' trials and place contractual limits on acceptable vibration levels. The vibration of primary concern is that occurring within habitable spaces, principally within deckhouses and engine rooms, and criteria are consequently based primarily on habitability standards. Limits on levels of equipment vibration, from an operability standpoint, are sometimes involved in specifications, particularly for naval vessels.

Most of the criteria established by the classification societies for commercial ships, which then reappear as limits in ship specifications, are at least consistent with Fig. 35, if not based directly upon it; ISO 6954 (1984) is a slightly more recent criteria of the same type. Figure 35, from SNAME (1980), is a plot of vibration response amplitude versus its frequency. The zones identified in Fig. 35 represent different levels of vibration severity; they are defined as follows.

Zone I—Vibration levels in this zone are low enough that adverse comments from personnel would not be expected.

Zone II—Vibration levels in this zone indicate that while vibration is noticeable, few adverse comments would be expected.
Zone III—In this zone, vibration levels and human response increase rapidly in severity and adverse comments would be expected.

The "response" of Fig. 35 can be chosen as displacement response, velocity response, or acceleration response, as indicated by the three different scales on the figure. For simple harmonic vibration, which Fig. 35 assumes, a simple relationship exists among the scales of displacement, velocity, and acceleration in Fig. 35. That is, for vibration displacement response at a point occurring as

$$x(t) = X \cos \omega t \qquad (172)$$

the displacement response amplitude is X. The velocity response, on the other hand, is, from equation (172),

$$v(t) = \dot{x}(t) = \omega X \cos(\omega t + \pi/2) \qquad (173)$$

The velocity response amplitude is therefore ωX, with ω being the vibratory frequency in radians per unit time. The acceleration response amplitude is similarly, $\omega^2 X$, by differentiation of formula (173).

As an example of the interchangeability, consider the vibration response corresponding to a displacement amplitude of $X = 1$ mm at a frequency of 5 Hz. The velocity amplitude is

$$X\omega = 1(5)2\pi = 31.4 \; mm \; per \; \sec$$

and the acceleration amplitude is

$$X\omega^2 = 1[(5)2\pi]^2 = 996 \; mm \; per \; \sec^2$$

Of course, these are all the same point in Fig. 35.

Velocity has replaced displacement in recent years as the popular unit for referring to ship vibration level. Full-power propeller blade-rate excitation frequency for the modern large ship is, for example, on the order of 10 Hz. Zone II of Fig. 35, whose vibration levels would be noticed by exposed personnel, has extremes of 4 and 9 mm/sec in the 10 Hz range. The vibration limits for habitable spaces imposed by most ship specifications seem generally to lie within this band.

For example, criteria that appear to have been adopted in a number of ship specifications, both naval and commercial, set an objective of 6.4 mm/sec and 3.8 mm/sec maximum vertical and horizontal, respectively, for vibration velocity of the hull girder. The design objective on major substructure maximum vibration, such as deckhouses, is 7.6 and 5.1 mm/sec vertical and horizontal, respectively. Note that all of these values fall within Zone II of Fig. 35, for typical propeller blade-rate

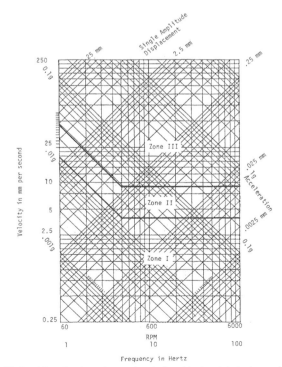

Fig. 35 Guidelines for ship vibration (vertical and horizontal, single amplitude).

frequencies. The criteria further recommend that maximum acceptable limits be set at 150% of the above values. The resulting vertical upper limits can then be seen to fall in lower Zone III in Fig. 35, with the corresponding horizontal limits falling in upper Zone II.

Figure 35, and other criteria like it, are readily applied when the vibration can be at least approximately characterized as simple harmonic (i.e., periodic at a single frequency). However, as noted in the last section, in general, ship vibration is not simple harmonic; it is not even periodic. Ship vibration is random (i.e., it is composed of components at all frequencies, rather than at a single one). The random character of ship vibration is clearly evident in records from underway vibration surveys. But the data from such complex records must often be compared with simple criteria, such as Fig. 35, to quantify its severity. ISO 6954 (2000) is a relatively new criteria expressed in terms of frequency-weighted root-mean-square (RMS) response levels, which is an attempt to account for randomness in the ship vibration record.

In propeller-excited ship vibration cases where cavitation is not heavily involved, propeller input spectra are narrow-band around blade-rate frequency, as mentioned in the last section. Furthermore, for structural resonance, or near resonance, at blade-rate frequency, the band of the vibration response spectra around the resonant frequency is further narrowed. In such cases, which are not uncommon, analog records unmistakably display a dominant blade-rate frequency characteristic. The RMS vibratory response amplitude is then usually evaluated from the records, either by "eyeball" or more precisely by spectral analysis, and matched with blade-rate frequency, as in equation (172), for comparison with the established limit criteria (see Fig. 35).

In the other extreme, where cavitation is heavily involved in nonresonant vibration, measured vibration records still usually exhibit a basically periodic character, but components at more than one discrete frequency are clearly evident. The component frequencies are the strong blade-rate multiples of the slowly convergent hull surface excitation associated with the cavitation intermittency. In this case, with significant component vibration occurring simultaneously at several different frequencies, it is not always clear how guidelines such as Fig. 35 are to be used. It is in such cases that criteria based on RMS level (i.e., ISO 6954, 2000) are the proper recourse.

A realistic and yet concise standard for the specification of propeller-induced ship vibration limits or criteria appears, in some respects, to be hardly less elusive than some parts of the design methodology needed to provide assurance in meeting such standards. Progress is, however, being made. A more recent interpretation of the zones of Fig. 35, according to (a) passenger cabins, (b) crew accommodations, and (c) working areas is presented in a matrix with the Discomfort Zones in ISO 6954 (2000). There, the velocity and acceleration amplitudes are specifically to be interpreted as RMS values to allow for the vibration not being simple harmonic.

4.2 Vibration Measurement

4.2.1 Design Verification. The SNAME Code for Shipboard Vibration Measurement (SNAME, 1975) recommends a very comprehensive program and instrumentation package for shipboard vibration surveys. The Code is invoked in many ship vibration specifications. An elaboration on the SNAME Code and proposal of a somewhat more advanced instrumentation package is that of de Bord, Hennessy, and McDonald (1998).

The instrumentation package proposed in the above SNAME Code has proved to be adequate in establishing compliance, or noncompliance, with the typical ship vibration specification. The instrumentation consists of a set of 12 inductance-type velocity pick-ups, with signal processing through an equal number of integrating amplifiers and with a permanent record of the resultant vibration displacement signature recorded graphically on a multichannel recorder. In providing the capability for simultaneous multipoint vibration measurement, this instrumentation can be used to establish vibration frequency, amplitude, and local relative displacement (mode shape). Evaluation of ship vibration for purposes of comparison against the typical specification will require the measurement of frequency and amplitude at the pre-established survey points, but not the phase relationships between points. Amplitude and frequency information can be obtained with acceptable accuracy using relatively simple portable instruments, with acceleration measurements at the survey points performed in some sequence, rather than simultaneously.

Of course, if the simple vibration survey of a new ship should establish that the specification limits are badly exceeded, then the type of measurement package proposed in SNAME (1975) may become absolutely essential to expeditious rectification. In this respect, invoking the SNAME Code, or its equivalent, in design specifications may be considered insurance worth the extra investment.

4.2.2 Posttrial Corrective Investigations. The approach to resolving a ship vibration problem, as with most engineering problems, involves two steps. The first step is to clearly establish the cause of the problem, and the second step is to implement the changes required to eliminate it in an efficient manner.

In about 80% of cases, the basic cause of a ship vibration problem is its propeller. This fact seems to be elusive to the vibration analyst familiar only with land-based power plant-oriented vibration problems; ship vibration is indeed a case of "the tail wagging the dog" most of the time. Whether or not the vibration of a particular ship has its source in the propeller is easily established from underway vibration measurements. If at some shaft RPM, the measured frequency of the vibration is predominantly RPM times propeller blade number, and varies directly with shaft RPM, then the propeller is definitely the exciting source. If blade-rate frequency, or its multiples, is not strongly detectable in the records, then it is almost certain that the propeller is not the primary excitation, unless the records exhibit a strong shaft-rate frequency, which could indicate propeller mechanical or hydrodynamic unbalance difficulties, but these are rather rare.

Once the excitation frequency has been established from the underway measurements, next is to establish whether resonance with structural natural frequencies plays a significant role in the magnitude of the vibration. For noncavitating propellers, excessive hull vibration should be expected to be resonant vibration. Resonant vibration is established by varying shaft RPM in steps and recording vibration amplitude successively at each RPM in the region where the problem has been identified as being most intense. If a plot of displacement amplitude versus RPM shows a definite peak with increasing RPM, followed by decline, then resonant vibration is established and the position of the peak establishes the natural frequency of the resonant structural mode. If the amplitude/RPM characteristic does not peak but has an increasing trend as roughly RPM squared in the upper power range, then structural resonance is not playing a major role. If, alternatively, the amplitude/RPM characteristic increases very rapidly only in the immediate vicinity of full power, without establishing a definite peak up to the maximum obtainable RPM, a full power resonance may or may not be indicated. This exhibition can be entirely the manifestation of the onset of propeller cavitation, which tends to produce almost discontinuous amplification of the hull surface excitation at the onset RPM. The sudden appearance of strong harmonics of blade-rate frequency in the vibration records, accompanied by violent pounding in spaces above the counter, are good indications of a full-power nonresonant vibration problem caused by excessive propeller cavitation.

If nonresonant vibration due to propeller cavitation is established, then the underway survey could probably be discontinued, with attention then turned to hydrodynamic design changes in the stern/propeller configuration. This course of action is considered in the next section.

If the problem is established as highly localized resonant vibration of plating panels, piping, and the like, then the vibration survey likewise need go no further. In such cases, it is usually quite obvious how natural frequency changes, through local stiffening, can be effectively and expediently accomplished to eliminate the locally resonant conditions.

If, on the other hand, the vibration problem is established as a resonant condition of a major substructure, such as a deckhouse, which has been all too often the case, then the vibration survey should proceed to obtain mode shape information in the interest of an expeditious correction program.

4.3 Posttrial Corrections. Just as in developing a vibration-sufficient ship design, all possibilities for correcting a vibration-deficient one are explicitly reflected in the general response formula (82) of Section 2. Practically speaking, there are three possibilities: (a) reduce vibratory excitation, (b) change natural frequencies to avoid resonance, or (c) change exciting frequencies to avoid resonance. Except in the rather uncommon case of excessive diesel engine-excited hull vibration, which can usually be corrected by moment compensators (Sulzer Bros., 1977) or engine resilient mounting (Anonymous, 1997), achievement of any of the three correction possibilities identified above will almost always involve modifications in either stern/propeller hydrodynamics or hull structure.

4.3.1 Hydrodynamic Modifications. The most effective way to reduce propeller vibratory excitation is to reduce the circumferential nonuniformity of the hull wake in which the propeller operates. In the design stage, acceptable wakes can be achieved by taking proper care with stern lines (see Section 3.7.) In a post-design corrective situation, basic lines changes are not possible. However, with good luck in the case of poor stern lines, considerable improvements in wake can be accomplished by back fitting one of the several types of wake adapting stern appendages. The partial tunnel (Fig. 36) has been the most broadly applied of the wake-adapting appendages, which also include vortex generators and wake-adapting propeller ducts. The partial tunnel was apparently first retrofitted for vibration reduction purposes by Baier and Ormondroyd (1952) on the laker Carl D. Bradley in 1951. The idea is to divert the upward flow along the buttock lines forward longitudinally into the upper propeller disc to reduce the wake spike near top dead-center. This device will work most effectively on the buttock-flow type of stern; the partial tunnel has been applied successfully over the years on the Great Lakes ore carriers, most of which have barge-type sterns with very steep buttock angles. On the other hand, for sterns which exhibit a basically waterline-flow character, the partial tunnel would be expected to be more or less ineffective due to the lack of upward flow to divert. However, the effectiveness of the partial tunnel cannot always be accurately judged by simply classifying a prospective application as one of the two limiting cases of buttock versus waterline flow. For example, the stern shown in Fig. 36, from Rutherford (1978–1979) might be classified as more of a waterline flow, yet the modifications shown produced significant improvement in the nominal wake, as exhibited by the before and after axial velocity contours. The Fig. 36 modifications, however, include vortex generators as well as the partial tunnel, and the contributions of each to the wake improvements shown are not known. A more direct indication of the effectiveness of the partial stern tunnel in reducing vibratory excitation is given in Fig. 37 and in Table 11, from Hylarides (1978). Figure 37 shows the stern lines of four ships on which partial stern tunnels were fitted as a result of posttrial corrective studies conducted at the Netherlands Ship Model Basin (NSMB). Pressures

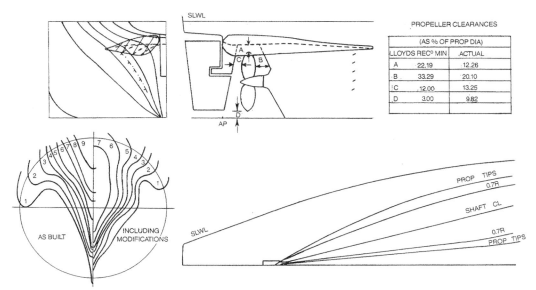

PROPELLER CLEARANCES

	(AS % OF PROP DIA)	
LLOYDS REC° MIN	.ACTUAL	
A	.22.19	.12.26
.B	33.29	.20.10
!C	.12.00	13.25
.D	3.00	9.82

Fig. 36 Wake improvement by means of special stern appendages, 7000-ton pallet cargo ship.

were measured on model sterns in the NSMB cavitation tunnel, integrated, and then harmonically analyzed to produce the first three harmonics of blade-rate vertical hull surface force. The force amplitudes, as percentages of steady thrust, are listed in Table 11 for each case. In the two cases where the outcome of the tunnel retrofit is indicated, the vibration was judged to be acceptable.

The force results of Table 11 for the two cases where measurements are listed both before and after the tunnel addition are surprising in one respect. In both cases, significant reductions in the second and third blade-rate amplitudes are attributed to the tunnels, but an increase

in the blade-rate forces is indicated. This is not impossible, yet it seems unlikely. In spite of the success of such model test programs in solving vibration problems associated with propeller hydrodynamics, it is difficult to have high confidence in the accuracy of force predictions of the type listed in Table 11. This is for the general reasons cited in Section 2. In view of the advances that are being made in the development of analytical/numerical hydrodynamic models, it seems certain that at some time in the future, hybrid schemes, exploiting the best features of numerical and experimental analysis, in combination, will be available to replace the purely

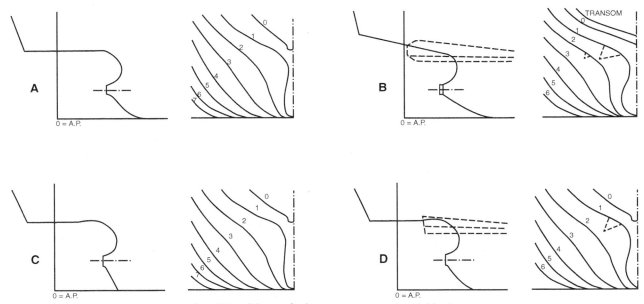

Fig. 37 Model sterns for force measurements (see Table 9).

Table 11 Vertical Surface Force Measurements on Models of Fig. 37

Ship Identification	Before Application of Partial Tunnel	After Application of Partial Tunnel	Application of Partial Stern Tunnel	Application of Partial Stern Tunnel
A	6.8/4.2	—	Unacceptable	Acceptable
	2.0/2.0*			
	1.9/0.5			
B	12.6	15.3	Unacceptable	Acceptable
	12.4	4.0		
	7.7	0.9		
C	32.7/12.1	—	Unacceptable	?
	13.6/14.6*			
	5.4/5.7			
D	28.0	41.9	Unacceptable	?
	6.9	3.4		
	4.4	1.4		

*Different propellers

experimental programs typical of that which produced the data of Table 11.

The decision to retrofit a wake-adapting stern appendage should not be made lightly without quantification of the advantages and disadvantages; a price is usually paid for appendages in increased hull resistance. As a minimum, model tuft-tests with and without the appendage should be performed to observe the change in stern surface flow. The absence of any noticeable smoothing may be misleading; however, a wake survey can show improvements in the propeller plane not discernible in the tuft behavior. Furthermore, aside from nominal wake considerations, it has been found that greatest wake improvements are sometimes achieved through propeller/appendage interaction (Hylarides, 1978). This implies that model tuft-tests should be conducted both with and without the operating propeller. In these cases, the best indicator of significant effective wake improvements from the standpoint of vibratory excitation may be an improvement, by several percentage points, in the propulsive efficiency from model SHP test conducted with and without the wake adapting appendage, as explained in Hylarides (1978).

Aside from wake improvements, the only recourse for reducing propeller excitation is modification or replacement of the propeller. Some instances of successful modifications of troublesome propellers have been reported. For example, trimming blade tips by several centimeters to reduce wake severity at the extreme propeller radii can produce improvements, but some degree of RPM increase must then be tolerated. Successful modifications of existing propellers are rare because of the usually unacceptable trade-offs of performance degradation against vibration improvement. The same disadvantages exist in propeller replacement considerations. Replacement propellers, with modified features such as changed blade number, reduced diameter (for increased hull clear-

ance), increased blade area, reduced pitch in the blade tips, etc., may relieve the vibration problem, but often for a dear price in vessel performance. It is unfortunate that, with the exception of blade skew, essentially all of the measures available in propeller design for reducing vibratory excitation, once the stern lines are established, act also to reduce propeller efficiency (refer to Chapter 5 for propeller design considerations). It cannot be emphasized strongly enough that the greatest insurance against propeller-induced vibration problems, and the persistent difficulties which then almost always ensue, is to place high emphasis on wake uniformity in making trade-offs in the original establishment of vessel lines.

4.3.2 Structural Modifications. The most cost-effective approach for eliminating structural resonances is usually to shift natural frequencies through structural modifications; the alternative is to shift exciting frequency by changes in engine RPM or number of propeller blades.

Just as with hydrodynamics-related problems, the most intelligent way to approach the correction of a vibration problem that promises to involve significant structural modifications is through the use of the tools of rational mechanics. A structural math model should first be calibrated to approximately simulate the existing vibration characteristics. Modification possibilities are then exercised with the model, and their probability of success is established on paper. In this way, the probability of a "one-shot" success when shipboard modifications are subsequently implemented is maximized. The alternative and unenlightened "cut-and-try" approach to the solution of serious ship vibration problems is fraught with frustration, and with the real possibility of expending vast amounts of time and money and never achieving complete success.

Of course, the paper-studies proposed as a tool for use in correcting a serious ship vibration problem must be concluded quickly; several months, or even several weeks, is not available when delivery of a vessel is stalled, awaiting the resolution of vibration deficiencies. This places a premium on formulation of the simplest possible structural models which still retain adequate realism to provide the basis for the required judgments as to the relative effects of vessel modifications. This is where the collection of thorough trial vibration data can pay for itself. Measurement of vibratory mode shape data is often a near necessity for securing guidance in formulating calibration models of the desired simplicity, but with sufficient accuracy. This is illustrated by the following simple example.

Assume that excessive vibration of a Type A deckhouse (see Fig. 20) occurs on the builder's trials of a vessel. Vibratory displacement amplitude data are recorded with phase-calibrated pick-ups mounted at points on the house and on the main deck. The records establish the following information.

1. The vibration occurs at predominantly blade-rate frequency, confirming the propeller as its exciting source.

2. The vibration amplitude peaks at 94 RPM, and the propeller has five blades. A resonance of the house at 470 cpm is therefore established.

3. Vibration recorded at 94 RPM show that the vibration of the house is predominantly fore-and-aft, with fore-and-aft amplitude increasing with a quasilinear characteristic from low levels at main deck to a maximum of 0.75 mm at the house top. The house top is 16 m above main deck.

4. The 100 RPM record also shows that the amplitude of the vertical vibration at main deck is approximately uniform at 0.1 mm over the house length. The vertical vibration amplitude is also approximately constant at this same level up the house front, which is a continuation of the forward engine room bulkhead.

The above characteristics are judged to allow the use of the simple rocking/bending house model in conjunction with the Hirowatari method (see Figs. 20 and 21 and Table 2 in Section 3).

4.3.3 Determination of Model Constants. For a Type A house with $h = 16$ m, the fixed-base fundamental house natural frequency is estimated from Fig. 21 as $f_\infty = 750$ cpm.

Using the Dunkerley formula, formula (135), with the measured house natural frequency $f_e = 470$ cpm, the effective rocking frequency is

$$f_R = \sqrt{\frac{1}{1/f_e^2 - 1/f_\infty^2}}$$

$$= 601 \text{ cpm} \tag{145}$$

The two frequencies f_∞ and f_R can be used to determine the effective stiffnesses of the house and its underdeck supporting structure for use in the simple model of Fig. 38.

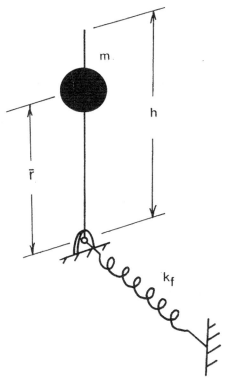

Fig. 38 Mass-elastic model of deckhouse and support structure.

For a house mass established as $m = 300$ t, with a radius of gyration, r, about the house forward lower edge of 10 m, the effective torsional stiffness of the underdeck supporting structure is, from equation (136),

$$K_f = (2\pi/60)^2 f_R^2 J$$

$$= 1.19 \times 10^{11} \text{ } N-m \text{ per rad} \tag{175}$$

where

$$J = m\bar{r}^2 = 3 \times 10^7 \text{ } kg-m^2$$

An approximate effective bending / shear stiffness of the house is obtained by first lumping the house mass at the radius of gyration above the assumed pin support on the main deck at the forward bulkhead; this preserves the mass moment of inertia in the Fig. 38 model. Then, for the house base fixed,

$$k_H = (2\pi/60)^2 f_\infty^2 m = 1.85 \times 10^9 \text{ } N \text{ per } m \tag{176}$$

The effective combined torsional stiffness for use in the equivalent reduced one-mass system of Fig. 39 is then

$$K = \frac{1}{1/K_f + 1/(k_H \bar{r}^2)}$$

$$= 0.724 \times 10^{11} \text{ } N-m \text{ per rad} \tag{177}$$

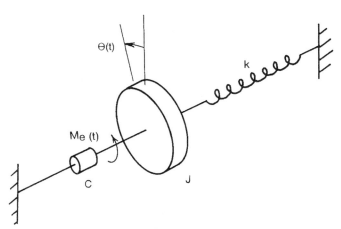

Fig. 39 Equivalent one-mass system.

This combined stiffness can also be deduced directly from the measured natural frequency and the house mass moment of inertia as

$$K = (2\pi/60)^2 f_e^2 J$$
$$= 0.724 \times 10^{11} N - m \; per \; rad \qquad (178)$$

The effective exciting moment due to the vertical hull girder vibration can be estimated using the formula developed in the simple rigid box deckhouse analysis of the second section. Referring to the development of formula (83), the amplitude of the exciting moment is

$$M_e = \omega^2 m \bar{\xi} X \qquad (179)$$

Here, $\bar{\xi}$ is the longitudinal coordinate to the house CG, measured aft from the house front, say, 5 m, and X is the 0.1 mm amplitude of the main deck vertical vibration. In terms of arbitrary hull girder vibration frequency ω,

$$M_e = 150 \; \omega^2 \; N - m \qquad (180)$$

The final remaining element of the Fig. 39 equivalent 1-mass model, the damping factor ζ, is estimated using the measured 0.75 mm house top vibration amplitude. With Θ being the amplitude of the equivalent vibratory rocking rotation angle of the house, the fore-and-aft displacement amplitude of the house top is approximated as

$$U = \Theta h$$

where h is the 16 m house height above main deck. Substituting the response formula for the Fig. 39 model, equation (94),

$$U = \frac{h M_e / K}{\sqrt{\left[1 - (\omega/\omega_n)^2\right]^2 + (2\zeta \omega/\omega_n)^2}} \qquad (181)$$

But at resonance, $\omega = \omega_n$, so that

$$U = \frac{h M_e / K}{2\zeta} \qquad (182)$$

or

$$\zeta = \frac{h M_e}{2 K U} \qquad (183)$$

For $\omega = \omega_n = 2\pi fe/60 = 49.1$ rad/sec in equation (180),

$$M_e = 3.62 \times 10^5 \, N - m$$

The damping factor is then, from equation (183),

$$\zeta = \frac{16 (3.62 \times 10^5)}{2 (0.724 \times 10^{11}) (0.75 \times 10^{-3})}$$
$$= 0.053 \qquad (184)$$

With the calibrated model so established as an equivalent one degree of freedom system, with constants, J, K, ζ, and M, the above formula can be reused to evaluate changes in the house-top vibratory displacement, U, resulting from selected changes in the array of design variables included in the simple formulation.

4.3.4 Structural Modifications. To demonstrate this procedure, assume that stiffening in the form of the added parallel pillars of the Section 3.4 and Fig. 22 examples are contemplated. Following that example, the torsional stiffness of the underdeck supporting structure is raised from the above value of 1.19×10^{11} Nm per radius to 1.33×10^{11} Nm per radius by the pillar addition. Resubstituting into equations (176) and (177), the increased combined stiffness of $K = 0.775 \times 10^{11}$ Nm per radius results in a 3.4% increase in natural frequency from the measured value of 469 cpm to 485 cpm.

Continuing with the scenario, assume that the full power RPM of the vessel is 98, which corresponds to a full power blade-rate exciting frequency of 490 cpm; the critical has therefore been raised only to a higher (more dangerous) level in the operating range (i.e., it has been raised from 94 to 97 RPM).

At 97 RPM, the 0.1 mm vertical hull girder vibration measured at 94 RPM would be increased by at least the frequency increase squared. This is assuming a flat frequency response characteristic of the hull girder (not close to a hull girder critical) as well as a noncavitating propeller. Assuming a frequency squared increase, the vertical hull girder vibration amplitude becomes

$$X = 0.1(97/94)^2 = 0.107 \; mm$$

with the exciting moment from equation (179) increasing to

$$M_e = 4.13 \times 10^5 \, N - m$$

at the new resonant frequency $\omega = \omega_n = (2\pi) (485/60) = 53.8$ radius/sec. The house top fore-and-aft vibratory displacement amplitude resulting from the foundation stiffening is changed, from equation (182), to

$$U = \frac{16 (4.13 \times 10^5)/0.775 \times 10^{11}}{2 (0.05)}$$
$$= 0.85 \, mm$$

This is an increase in vibration of 13% over the original 0.75 mm level! The inadequate stiffening has simply raised the critical to a higher point in the operating range where the excitation is more intense. Some care is required here in order to achieve a satisfactory result.

It would be intelligent at this point to evaluate the stiffness increase required in order to achieve a satisfactory vibration level. It is necessary to move the critical above the full power RPM of 98. This establishes the exciting frequency at the full power RPM

$$f = 490 \ cpm = 8.17 \ Hz$$

$$\omega = 8.17 \ (2\pi) = 51.3 \ rad \ per \ sec$$

On consulting Fig. 35, a limiting house-top fore-and-aft vibratory velocity amplitude of 5 mm per second is selected at this frequency. This corresponds to a house-top displacement amplitude

$$U = 5/\omega = 0.097 \ mm$$

The exciting moment, for use in formula (181), continuing to assume a frequency squared variation in the hull vertical displacement amplitude, is now, from equation (179),

$$M_e = (51.3)^2(3 \times 10^5)(5)(.1)(98/94)^2/1000$$
$$= 4.31 \times 10^5 \ N - m$$

From equation (181), for $2\zeta\omega/\omega_n \ll [\ 1 - (\omega/\omega_n)^2]$ for $\omega/\omega_n < 1$,

$$U = \frac{hMe/K}{1-(\omega/\omega_n)^2} \qquad (185)$$

Then, with $\omega_n = \sqrt{K/J}$,

$$K = hMe/U + J\omega^2 \qquad (186)$$

Substituting the values, the required combined stiffness is

$$K = 1.50 \times 10^{11} \ N - m \ per \ rad$$

This requires more than doubling the as-built combined effective stiffness of 0.724×10^{11} Nm per radius (equation [177]).

Little can normally be done to change the house stiffness; functional requirements of the house usually will not permit the modifications necessary to accomplish any significant increases in house casing section moment of inertia and shear area. Assume that stiffening of the underdeck supporting structure is the only possibly effective structural modification that can be accommodated. The required K_f is, using equation (178),

$$K_f = \frac{1}{1/K - 1/K_H \bar{r}^2} = 7.87 \times 10^{11} \ N - m \ per \ rad$$

Therefore, meeting the vibration limit of 5 mm/sec at the house-top will require increasing the torsional stiffness of the underdeck supporting structure by a factor of

$$\frac{7.87 \times 10^{11}}{1.19 \times 10^{11}} = 6.6$$

and this would be impossible in any real case. For example, if the two parallel pillars of the example in Section 3.4 were doubled in number from 2 to 4 and moved 3 m aft to line up under the house after bulkhead, rather than under the house sides (see Fig. 22), K_f would be increased to only

$$K_f = 1.19 \times 10^{11} + 2(4 \times 10^8)(8)^2$$
$$= 1.70 \times 10^{11} \ N - m \ per \ rad$$

which is still a factor of more almost 5 below the required value.

At this point, the virtual impossibility of rectifying the problem through structural modifications should be clear, and attention would be turned to ordering a new propeller.

4.3.5 A Propeller Change. Considering an alternative four-bladed propeller, the critical would be shifted to

$$94(5/4) = 117.5 \ RPM$$

which is well beyond the operating range. With the foundation unchanged, the house-top vibration at the full power RPM of 98 would be, from equation (185),

$$U = \frac{16(4.31 \times 10^5)/0.724 \times 10^{11}}{1-(98/117.5)^2} \times 1000$$
$$= 0.313 \ mm$$

which assumes an unchanged propeller excitation level. The new house-top displacement corresponds to a velocity amplitude of

$$0.313(41.05) = 12.84 \ mm/sec$$

This would probably not be acceptable, on the basis of Fig. 35.

Another possibility for the propeller would be to change to six blades and lower the critical well below full power to

$$94(5/6) = 78.3 \ RPM$$

At full power in this case

$$U = \frac{16(4.31 \times 10^5)/0.724 \times 10^{11}}{|1-(98/78.3)^2|} \times 1000$$
$$= 0.168 \ mm$$

and the velocity is

$$0.168(98/6) = 2.74 \ mm/sec$$

This would be clearly acceptable, by Fig. 35. The potential disadvantage to six blades is the resonance at 78 RPM.

At 78 RPM, the exciting moment, equation (179), should be down by at least frequency squared (which ignores any reduction at all in the hull girder vibration level).

$$M_e = 4.31 \times 10^5 (78.3/98)^2 = 2.75 \times 10^5 \, N-m$$

so that the resonant amplitude should be, at most, from equation (182),

$$U = \frac{16(2.75 \times 10^5)/0.724 \times 10^{11}}{2(0.05)} \times 1000$$
$$= 0.608 \, mm$$

For

$$f = 6(78.3)/60 = 7.83 \, Hz \, and$$

$$\omega = 2\pi f = 49.2 \, rad \, per \, sec$$

the vibratory velocity amplitude would be

$$0.608(49.2) = 29.9 \, mm \, per \, sec$$

While this level is excessive (see Fig. 35), it would not necessarily disqualify a six-bladed propeller, as continuous operation at any particular lower RPM is not usually critical, and 83 RPM could be simply avoided except in passing.

This example, which is from an actual case history, does demonstrate effectively the real danger of designing and building a vibration problem into a ship and the difficulty in removing it.

References

American Bureau of Shipping. (2006). *ABS guidance notes on ship vibration*. Houston, TX: ABS.

Anonymous. (1997). Rigid or flexible engine mountings? *The Naval Architect*, 4, 43–44.

Baier, L. A., & Ormondroyd, J. (1952). Vibration at the Stern of Single Screw Vessels. SNAME Spring Meeting, New Orleans, LA, May.

Beck, R., & Reed, A. (2010). *Seakeeping*. Jersey City, NJ: SNAME.

Beranek, L. (1960). *Noise reduction*. New York: McGraw-Hill.

Bobrovnitskii, Y. I. (2001). Models of acoustic sources: a survey. *Proceedings Internoise 2001*, The Hague, Holland.

Boswell, R. J., Kim, K.-H., Jessup, S. D., & Lin, G. F. (1983). Practical methods for predicting periodic propeller loads. Report 83/090, *DTNSRDC*, October.

Bourceau, G., & Volcy, G. C. (1970). Forced vibration resonators and free vibration of the hull. *Bulletin Technique du Bureau Veritas*, April–July.

Breslin, J. P. (1959). A theory for the vibratory effects produced by a propeller on a large plate. *Journal of Ship Research*, 3.

Breslin, J. P. (1970). Theoretical and experimental techniques for practical estimation of propeller-induced vibratory forces. *SNAME Transactions*, 78.

Breslin, J. P., & Kowalski, T. (1964). Experimental study of propeller-induced vibratory pressures on simple surfaces and correlation with theoretical predictions. *Journal of Ship Research*, 8.

Bureau Veritas. (1979). Recommendations designed to limit the effects of vibrations onboard ships. *Bureau Veritas Guidance Note Nl 138-A-RD3*, June.

Burrill, L. C. (1934–1935). Ship vibration: Simple methods of estimating critical frequencies. *Trans NECI*, 51.

Cox, G. G., & Morgan, W. B. (1972). The use of theory in propeller design. *SNAME*, Chesapeake Section, February.

Cumming, R. A., Morgan, W. B., & Boswell, R. J. (1972). Highly skewed propellers. *SNAME Transactions*, 80.

de Bord, F., Hennessy, W., & McDonald, J. (1998). Measurement and analysis of shipboard vibrations. *Marine Technology*, 35, 1–9.

de Jong, C. A. F., & de Regt, M. J. A. M. (1998). Prediction of propeller cavitation noise on board ships. In W. C. Oosterveld, & S. G. Tan (Eds.), *Practical design of ships and mobile units* (pp. 919–925). Maryland Heights, MO: Elsevier Science.

DenHartog, J. P. (1956). *Mechanical vibrations* (4th ed.). Columbus, OH: McGraw-Hill.

Denny, S. B. (1967). Comparisons of experimentally determined and theoretically predicted pressures in the vicinity of a marine propeller. *NSRDC Report 2349*, May.

Dyne, G. (1974). A study on the scale effect of wake, propeller cavitation, and vibratory pressure at hull of two tanker models. *SNAME Transactions*, 82.

Gesret, V. (2000). Propeller noise calculation based on full-scale measurements. *Proceedings Internoise 2000*, Nice, France.

Hadler, J. B., & Cheng, H. M. (1965). Analysis of experimental wake data in way of propeller plane of single and twin screw ship models. *SNAME Transactions*, 73.

Hammer, N. O., & McGinn, R. F. (1978). Highly skewed propellers-full scale vibration test results and economic considerations. *Ship Vibration Symposium '78*, Washington, DC, October.

Harrington, R. L. (1992). *Marine engineering*. Jersey City, NJ: SNAME.

Hirowatari, T., & Matsumoto, K. (1969). On the fore-and-aft vibration of superstructure located at aftship (Second Report). *JSNA Transactions*, 125.

Holden, K. O., Fagerjold, O., & Ragnar, F. (1980). Early design-stage approach to reducing hull surface forces due to propeller cavitation. *SNAME Transactions*, 88.

Huang, T., & Groves, N. (1981). Effective wake: Theory and experiment. *DTNSRDC Report 81/033*, April.

Hylarides, S. (1978). Some hydrodynamic considerations of propeller-induced ship vibrations. *Ship Vibration Symposium '78*, Washington, DC, October.

ISO 6954 (2000). Mechanical vibration: Guidelines for the measurement, reporting and evaluation of vibration with regard to habitability on passenger and merchant ships. Geneva, Switzerland: ISO.

Johannessen, H., & Skaar, K. T. (1980). Guidelines for prevention of excessive ship vibration. *SNAME Transactions, 88*.

Kagawa, K. (1978). A study on higher mode vibration of ships (1st Report). *Journal of JSNA, 143*.

Kennard, E. H. (1955). Forced vibrations of beams and the effect of sprung masses. *DTMB Report 955*, July.

Kinsler, L. E., & Frey, A. R. (1962). *Fundamentals of acoustics* (2nd ed.). New York: Wiley.

Krylov, A. N. (1936). *Vibration of ships* (in Russian). Moscow, Russia: ONTI.

Kumai, T. (1968). On the estimation of natural frequencies of vertical vibration of ships. *Report of Research Institute for Applied Mechanics, 16*.

Lee, C.-S. (1979). *Prediction of steady and unsteady performance of marine propellers with or without cavitation by numerical lifting surface theory* (Doctoral dissertation). Massachusetts Institute of Technology, Cambridge, MA.

Lewis, F. M. (1929). The inertia of water surrounding a vibrating ship. *SNAME Transactions, 37*.

Lewis, F. M. (1963). Propeller-vibration forces. *SNAME Transactions, 71*.

Lewis, F. M. (1973). Propeller excited hull and rdder force measurements. *Department of Ocean Engineering, MIT Report 73-10*.

McCarthy, J. H. (1961). On the calculation of thrust and torque fluctuations of propellers in non-uniform wake flow. *DTMB Report 1533*.

Pien, P. C. (1958). Five hole spherical pitot tube. *DTMB Report 1229*, May.

Pollard, T., & Dudebout, A. (1894). *Theorie du Navire* (Vol. IV, Chapter LXIX). Paris: Gauthier Villars & Fils.

Reed, F. E. (1971). The design of ships to avoid propeller excited vibrations. *SNAME Transactions, 79*.

Rutherford, R. (1978–1979). Aft end shaping to limit vibration. *North East Coast Institution of Engineers and Shipbuilders Transactions, 95*.

Sandstrom, R. E., & Smith, N. P. (1979). Eigenvalue analysis as an approach to the prediction of global vibration of deckhouse structures. *SNAME Hampton Roads Section Meeting*, October.

Sasajima, H., & Tanaka, I. (1966). On estimation of wake of ships. *Proceedings 11th ITTC*, Tokyo.

Schlick, O. (1884–1911). Series of articles on ship vibration in transactions, INA (1884, 1893, 1894, 1901, 1911).

Schlottmann, G., Winkelmann, J., & Sideris, D. (1999). Vibrations of resilient mounted engines [in German]. *Jahrbuch der Schiffbautechnischen Gesellschaft, 93*, 185–193.

Schlottmann, G., Winkelmann, J., Weihert, J., Großmann, S., & Sideris, D. (2000a). Dynamic behaviour of resiliently mounted engines considering vibration excitation and characteristics of spring elements [in German]. *Schiffbauforschung, 39*, 15–42.

Schlottmann, G., Winkelmann, J., Weihert, J., Großmann, S., Sideris, D., & Weidner, U. (2000b). Program for prediction of dynamic behaviour of resiliently mounted engines [in German]. *FDS/Hamburg, University of Rostock Report No. 290*.

Sellers, M. L., & Kline, R. G. (1967). Some aspects of ship stiffness. *Transactions SNAME, 75*, 268–295.

SNAME. (1975). Code for shipboard hull vibration measurements. *T&R Code C-1*, January.

SNAME. (1980). Ship vibration and noise guidelines. *Technical and Research Bulletin, 2*, January.

Stern, F., & Vorus, W. S. (1983). A nonlinear method for predicting unsteady sheet cavitation on marine propellers. *Journal of Ship Research*, March.

Stuntz, G. R., Pien, P. C., Hinterthan, W. B., & Ficken, N. L. (1960). Series 60-The effects of variations in afterbody shape upon resistance, power, wake distribution, and propeller excited vibratory forces. *SNAME Transactions, 68*.

Sulzer Bros. (1977). *RND. Marine diesel engines, technical data*. Sulzer Bros. Ltd., Winterthur, Switzerland, October.

Tanibayashi, H. (1980). Practical approach to unsteady problems of marine propellers by quasi-steady method of calculation. *Mitsubishi Technical Bulletin, 143*.

Thomson, W. T. (1973). *Theory of vibration with applications*. Upper Saddle River, NJ: Prentice Hall.

Todd, F. H. (1935). Vibration of ships. *Tekniska Samfundets Handlinger No. 5*, Gøteborg, Sweden.

Todd, F. H. (1961). *Ship hull vibration*. London: Edward Arnold, Ltd.

Troost, L. (1937–1951). Open water test series with modern propeller forms. Part I, *Transactions NECI*, 1937–1938; Part II, 1939–1940; Part III, 1950–1951.

Tsakonas, S., Breslin, J., & Miller, M. (1967). Correlation and application of an unsteady flow theory for propeller forces. *SNAME Transactions, 75*, 158–193.

von Karman, T., & Sears, W. R. (1938). Airfoil theory for non-uniform motion. *Journal of the Aeronautical Sciences, 5*, August.

Vorus, W. S. (1971). An integrated approach to the determination of propeller generated forces acting on a ship hull. *Department of Naval Architecture and Marine Engineering, The University of Michigan, Report #072*, March.

Vorus, W. S. (1974). A method for analyzing the propeller induced vibratory forces acting on the surface of a ship stern. *SNAME Transactions, 82*, 186–210.

Vorus, W. S. (1976). Calculation of propeller induced hull forces, force distributions, and pressures; free-surface effects. *Journal of Ship Research, 20*, June.

Vorus, W. S., Breslin, J. P., & Tein, Y. S. (1978). Calculation and comparison of propeller unsteady pressure forces on ships. *Ship Vibration Symposium '78*, Washington, DC, October.

Vorus, W. S., & Hylarides, S. (1981). The hydrodynamic mass matrix of a vibrating ship based on a distribution of hull surface sources. *SNAME Transactions, 89.*

Vorus and Associates (1981). Analysis of propeller cavitation and propeller induced vibratory forces and pressures on a U.S. naval oiler. *Second Report VA181-2*, September.

Ward, G. (1982). The application of current vibration technology in routine ship design work. *RINA Spring Meeting Transactions.*

Wilson, M. B. (1981). Review of available criteria for identifying the likelihood of excessive propeller induced excitation. *DTNSRDC Report SPD-1001-01*, May.

INDEX